YOUR **CONFIRMATION** BIBLE COMPANION

Dear Abby,

I am so excited for you on your Confirmation! Now that you are armed with the Holy Spirit, I look forward to seeing what the Lord will do with your discipleship! Let the adventure begin!!

With love from your brother in Christ,

KP

YOUR
CONFIRMATION
BIBLE
COMPANION

What Scripture as "God's Love Song" Means for You

KEVIN DOWD

TWENTY-THIRD PUBLICATIONS
twentythirdpublications.com

DEDICATION

This book is dedicated to my dad,
John F. Dowd Sr.,
who passed away from Parkinson's disease on March 24, 2020.

Flame of warmth and brilliant light,
You have set me afire;
To be like you, to set others aflame:
This is my great desire.

SPECIAL THANKS

A special thank you to my 15-year-old nephew,
Paul B. Dowd Jr.,
who read every chapter and gave me feedback.
The book is better because of his insights.
Any mistakes in the book are, of course, my own.

DEDICATED THIS PENTECOST SUNDAY, MAY 31, 2020

TWENTY-THIRD PUBLICATIONS
One Montauk Avenue, Suite 200 · New London, CT 06320
(860) 437-3012 or (800) 321-0411 · www.twentythirdpublications.com

ISBN: 978-1-62785-565-5 · Cover art: Maike Hildebrandt/Shutterstock.com
Printed in the U.S.A.

A division of Bayard, Inc.

Contents

The Bible Is God's Love Song

"That is why the Lord gives you his word, so that you can receive it like a love letter he has written to you, to help you realize that he is at your side." **POPE FRANCIS**

A letter from Almighty God. That's what Pope St. Gregory the Great called the Bible. Pope Leo XIII called it "a Letter, written by our heavenly Father." And more recently, Pope Francis referred to it as a love letter. In many ways the Bible is like a love letter, but it is a lyrical love letter. It is like a love song. Love songs are full of metaphors and symbols. For example, we don't really "fall" when we fall in love, but we know what it means. We don't really have butterflies in our stomach. Our hearts don't really stop, and they aren't really on fire. There isn't really a spark between us, and when we think someone is "hot" we don't mean anything about their temperature. God's love song is like this. We don't read the Bible literally, as if it were a history book or a science textbook. It isn't like that. It's more like a song where the meaning is more important than the words. And the meaning—no matter what crazy words are sometimes used—is always about God's love for us and our invitation to freely respond by loving God and one another.

The Bible is an inspired collection of writings written over a long period of time. Christians believe the Holy Spirit inspired human authors and editors to write and collect the books of the Bible. "The Bible is not a book," Bishop Barron of Los Angeles reminds us. "It is a library." There are many books gathered together into the Bible: 46 books in the Old Testament and 27 books in the New Testament. Each book was written at a different time by different human authors, who were free to use different styles, genres, and languages. Since they were free, the Bible even includes their human prejudices, foibles, and sins. What holds it all together? It is all part of the same love song. It is all part of the story of God revealing more and more of Godself to us, so that we can know God. Knowing God, we fall in love with God. Falling in love, we want to show our love by doing something—serving God and one another. In other words, the love song is call-and-response. It is a wooing!

Since the Bible represents God's self-revelation over a long period of time, Christians believe that we can only understand the earlier writings once God fully revealed Godself in Christ and gave us the Holy Spirit. The Spirit gives us the gifts of Knowledge, Wisdom, and Understanding, which we need to make sense of the love song. Origen, an early Church Father, told us that we should read all of the Bible from the perspective of the last book of the Bible. In other words, once God had revealed everything in Christ, then we can make sense of the earlier writings.

This process of slowly revealing Godself to us has a name. We call it the *pedagogy of God*. That's just a fancy term that means God was teaching us little bits at a time over the centuries. It's actually a lot like school. I used to teach seventh-grade math. The way I taught math, though, was never meant just to give my students a seventh-grade education. I was preparing them for eighth-grade math and beyond. Also, I knew they would come into my class having a good understanding of sixth-grade math. Imagine if a student arrived in my class and didn't even know how to form numbers or how to add and subtract or what an equation was? That never happened, though, because they had learned their numbers and how to count when they were very young, and then they learned about equations and arithmetic in the lower grades. By the time they reached middle school, we could begin algebra, graphing equations, and figuring out percentages and complicated word problems.

In a similar way, step by step through the centuries, God revealed more to us, preparing us ultimately for God's full revelation when God became one of us—Jesus. Jesus is God in the flesh. Everything in the Bible is about Jesus, either by preparing us for him or telling us about him. In math class, there were things you could leave behind once you moved on to the next level. Your homework looked way different in seventh grade than in first grade. There was no need to go back to that first-grade work either. You had learned it—you were ready to move on. In the same way, some things in the Old Testament involve ideas about God and religious practices that we don't follow anymore. They served their purpose back then. They prepared us for Christ.

That's not to say the Old Testament isn't important. It's still the word of God! In the early years of Christianity, a man named Marcion rejected the entire Hebrew Bible, which we call the Old Testament. He thought that the God it talked about was a false god and not the same God that Jesus called his Father. But it is the same God! It's just that we were still learning more and more about God. And besides, the Hebrew Bible is what Jesus studied, prayed with, and taught from. To reject it would mean rejecting Jesus and rejecting our Jewish roots. Jesus was Jewish! Mary was Jewish! The Apostles were Jewish! The Church wisely used its teaching authority to reject Marcionism. To this day, the Catholic Bible includes Christian writings (New Testament) and Jewish writings (Old Testament). We consider both to be inspired by the Holy Spirit. And we honor our Jewish brothers and sisters to this day not only for the heritage they left to us, but for their ongoing faith in the God who chose to break into history and sing us a love song.

"What is Scripture,
if not a letter from Almighty
God? The Lord of [humans]
and of angels, has sent
you his letters for your life's
advantage—and yet you neglect
to read them eagerly! Study them,
I beg you, and meditate daily
on the words of your creator.
**LEARN THE HEART OF GOD
IN THE WORDS OF GOD."**

POPE ST. GREGORY THE GREAT

Part I

THE MEANING
of the LOVE SONG

"Catholics believe that the key that opens up and gives coherence to the many words contained in the Bible is Jesus [who is himself] the Word of God. Because God has spoken to us in Jesus the Word made flesh, we can understand and appreciate the words of the Bible. In this sense Christianity is only secondarily a religion of the book. It is primarily the religion of a person, Jesus the Word of God." **FR. DANIEL HARRINGTON, SJ**

"St. John said: 'I write to you, young people, because you are strong and the word of God abides in you' (1 John 2:14). Seeking the Lord, keeping his word, entrusting our life to him and growing in the virtues: all these things make young hearts strong. That is why you need to stay connected to Jesus, to 'remain online' with him, since you will not grow happy and holy by your own efforts and intelligence alone. Just as you try not to lose your connection to the internet, make sure that you stay connected to the Lord." **POPE FRANCIS**

CHAPTER 1

Who's Singing This??

"All divine Scripture speaks of Christ, and all divine Scripture is fulfilled in Christ."
HUGH OF ST. VICTOR, *CATECHISM OF THE CATHOLIC CHURCH* (CCC), 134

D id you ever hear a new song that is amazing, but you don't know who the artist is? No matter how good the song is, we're usually not satisfied until we find out who sings it. It matters to us whose voices we're hearing and who's in the band. And then, once we find out, what happens next? We start listening to their other music, right? We want to know if they have other great songs. And maybe we learn more about the group by talking to our friends, reading stories, or watching videos. Suddenly, the song we liked makes even more sense. Knowing the singer and songwriter can make a big difference.

Reading the Bible is something like hearing a new song. It makes a lot more sense to us if we know the singer. In the case of the Bible, the songwriter is the Father. The singer is the Holy Spirit, whom we receive in Confirmation. And the whole song is about Jesus! In fact, everything in the Bible is a partial revelation until we get to Jesus, who is the full revelation of God. We learn that "God is love" (1 John 4:8). The whole Bible exists for us to develop a loving relationship with Jesus and one another.

The Bible is like God's love song to the world. God is madly in love with all that God created. There is nothing God desires more from us than a loving relationship. But how do we love someone we don't know? In the Bible, we see God's self-revelation over time. We witness the people (Jews at first, then also Christians) getting to know God better over the centuries. It leads up to the ultimate revelation: God, without losing anything divine, becomes "incarnate of the Virgin Mary." This means that God became one of us. Jesus is "true God from true God" but also "like us in all things but sin." He is the fullness of God's self-revelation. Jesus is God in the flesh. In Jesus, we know God. In Jesus, we also know what a perfectly loving human being is. God's love for the world is fully accepted by Jesus on behalf of all humankind, and fully reciprocated without any sin or selfishness—even to the death. This is the love song of the Bible. It is a call-and-response song. We are invited into the story.

So where should I start my reading of the Bible? Since the singer is the Holy Spirit and the song is all about Jesus, we begin by asking the Spirit for the gift of Knowledge. We want to know Jesus, and in knowing Jesus, we know God. Since the whole Bible is about Jesus, we need to know him in order to read everything correctly. "Because we are Christian, we begin with Jesus," says catechist Catherine Maresca. Bad and even dangerous interpretations arise when we forget that the story is all about Jesus and God's love. So pray for the gift of Knowledge, and then start reading the Bible with the gospels: Matthew, Mark, Luke, and John. The gospels introduce us to Jesus. Mark is the shortest and the oldest. That's a good place to begin. Once we know Jesus better, we'll understand the whole love song so much better too.

Praying with the Bible

■ INVITE THE HOLY SPIRIT

Come, O Holy Spirit, and bless me with the gift of Knowledge. I desire
to know Jesus in a more personal way. I want to become friends with
the Lord and to love what he loves. I want to see how all of Scripture points
to him and how he taught us to respond to God's love with love. I want to
know the love song. I want to know it by heart! *(Pause in silence.) (Now read
the passage…)*

> *[Jesus] said to them, "How foolish you are, and how slow to believe
> all that the prophets have spoken! Did not the Messiah have to
> suffer these things and then enter his glory?" And beginning with
> Moses and all the Prophets, he explained to them what was said in
> all the Scriptures concerning himself.* LUKE 24:25-27

■ TALK TO JESUS

Now, talk to Jesus as a friend, in your own words, from your heart. Express
your desire to know him better, more personally. Although he knows you
perfectly and loves you unconditionally, Jesus still loves to have you reveal
yourself too. Share what's on your mind. Share your hopes and dreams. Share
your fears and anxieties. Share your broken heart or your heart bursting with
love. Jesus understands it all, for he is "like us in all things but sin." He cares
deeply about even the smallest things that are on our minds and hearts.

■ GIVE GLORY TO THE FATHER

The Father did not want Jesus to suffer and die a torturous death. Sinful
people wanted that. What pleased the Father was that Jesus' love was so
unselfish, so perfect, that he was willing to be killed rather than stop loving.
He could have used violence to prevent his own death. He chose love. That
love is what saves us, for "love covers a multitude of sins" (1 Peter 4:8). Give
glory to the Father for sending us a Savior who showed us what perfect love
looks like.

Confirmed in the Faith

QUESTIONS TO HELP US GROW STRONGER

Pick one or two questions to reflect on as you think about the meaning of your Confirmation and life in the Spirit.

- How can I unwrap the gift of Knowledge that the Holy Spirit gives in Confirmation, so that I will know God better?

- What does it mean to say that God's love song is call-and-response?

- Catholic theologians say we should read the whole Bible with a "Christological lens." This means having the same vision as Jesus. What does this mean to you personally?

- St. Jerome said, "Ignorance of Scripture is ignorance of Christ." What do you think he meant? Do you think the opposite may be true as well, that ignorance of Christ leads to ignorance of Scripture?

My Bible Journal

A SPACE FOR PERSONAL REFLECTIONS

_____

_____

_____

_____

_____

"So we come to know Christ and this knowledge becomes the main source of a firm understanding of the truth of all sacred Scripture." **ST. BONAVENTURE**

"The parts of Scripture are like tiles of a mosaic and should together form an image of the King." **ST. IRENAEUS OF LYONS**

CHAPTER 2

What Does It Mean??

*"[The Lord] has hidden in his word all treasures, so that each
of us may find a richness in what he or she contemplates."* **ST. EPHREM**

"Christ frees us from the slavery of the letter…"
CARDINAL JOSEPH RATZINGER (FUTURE POPE BENEDICT XVI)

Have you ever heard a new song and immediately looked up the lyrics to try to figure out what it means? According to LyricFind, this happened a lot with the crossover song "Old Town Road." But the lyrics only get us part way there, right? Once we know for sure what the words are, we begin to dig deeper. We watch the music video for more clues. Perhaps we look up interviews with the singers and songwriters. We really want to know what it means. We talk to our friends. We look online. We want to know the meaning of the symbols, metaphors, and figures of speech. We're beginning to interpret the song. The metaphors in the song mix with the experiences in our life and the information we gathered to generate a meaning.

Scripture is very much like this. Catholics do not read the Bible literally. We don't believe God spoke and some ancient person transcribed it, as if it were Divine Dictation. We don't think that the words alone are enough to hear what God is saying. We go deeper. We want to know the meaning. We expect to find symbolism, metaphors, and imagery of all sorts. We expect to have to do some thinking. Faith and reason work together after all.

Because Scripture is far more than just the literal text, the Bible is infinitely rich in meaning. This is what St. Ephrem was talking about in the quote above. Scripture is like a good song that reveals more and more depth and meaning the more you contemplate it. And, like a good song, it will have new meanings at different stages of life.

Why is this? Because God is speaking—present tense! If it were just the words on the page that mattered, that would be like saying God spoke—past tense—and we're lucky somebody wrote it down. Catholics don't believe that. We believe that it is a living word (see Hebrews 4:12). As the late, brilliant Scripture scholar Fr. Daniel Harrington, SJ, wrote, "The 'word of God' is not identical with the text of the Bible. For me, it refers to the whole process of encountering God in and through the Scriptures." He says, "In the encounter between the reader and the text, the 'word of God' comes alive" (*How Can I find God?*). This is why Pope Benedict reminded us of St. Jerome's words: "The Bible is the means 'by which God speaks daily to believers.'" In other words, in the Bible we don't encounter a dead text, but we encounter the living God!

A song comes alive in the encounter too. It's why no two people hear the same song the same way. When we leave behind the literalism that treats Scripture as dead words on a page, we open up to the encounter in which God speaks a living, personal word. Instead of getting stuck on the text, which gets us stuck in the past, we move into the realm of meaning, which is relevant today. What gift of the Holy Spirit helps us to do this? The gift of Understanding!

Praying with the Bible

🔢 INVITE THE HOLY SPIRIT

Come, O Holy Spirit, and grant me the gift of Understanding, so that I may find riches in contemplating the Scriptures with all the metaphors and meaning hidden in them. Help me to hear the living word speaking to me today. (*Pause in silence.*) (*Now read the passage...*)

> *The disciples approached him and said, "Why do you speak to them in parables?" He said to them in reply, "Because knowledge of the mysteries of the kingdom of heaven has been granted to you, but to them it has not been granted. To anyone who has, more will be given and he will grow rich; from anyone who has not, even what he has will be taken away. This is why I speak to them in parables, because 'they look but do not see and hear but do not listen or understand.'"* MATTHEW 13:10-13

🔢 TALK TO JESUS

Now, talk to Jesus as a friend, in your own words, from your heart. Share with him what confuses you and what you don't understand. Like the disciples, don't be afraid to ask Jesus questions. Ask him to help you to understand the deeper meaning of the Bible.

🔢 GIVE GLORY TO THE FATHER

Jesus said the difference between those who understood the parables and those who did not was "knowledge of the mysteries of the kingdom of heaven." The Church teaches us that this knowledge is first and foremost knowledge of a person, Jesus Christ. The disciples really knew Jesus, and so they understood the "mysteries." The crowds only knew *about* Jesus. It's like having a teacher who knows your name but doesn't really bother to get to know the real you. We shouldn't be like that teacher with other people or with Jesus. Make a decision to get to know Jesus better, more personally. The more we know him, the more we love him. The more we love him, the more we want to be like him. The more we are like him, the more the Father is glorified because we have chosen the Way of perfect love!

Confirmed in the Faith

QUESTIONS TO HELP US GROW STRONGER

Pick one or two questions to reflect on as you think about the meaning of your Confirmation and life in the Spirit.

- Do I really know Jesus, or do I only know *about* Jesus?

- Do I love Jesus and want to become more like him?

- When I read the Bible, do I listen for the living word of God speaking to the Church today through the Holy Spirit, or do I take every word on the page literally?

- Am I willing to open the gift of Understanding that the Holy Spirit gives in Confirmation so that my reading of Scripture draws me closer to Christ?

My Bible Journal

A SPACE FOR PERSONAL REFLECTIONS

_____

_____

"If the Scriptures are not to remain a dead letter, Christ, the eternal Word of the living God, must, through the Holy Spirit, 'open [our] minds to understand the Scriptures.'" **CATECHISM OF THE CATHOLIC CHURCH (CCC) 108**

"Indeed, to arrive at a completely valid interpretation of words inspired by the Holy Spirit, one must first be guided by the Holy Spirit and it is necessary to pray for that, to pray much, to ask in prayer for the interior light of the Spirit and docilely accept that light, to ask for the love that alone enables one to understand the language of God who 'is love' (1 Jn 4:8, 16)." **POPE ST. JOHN PAUL II**

CHAPTER 3

It's More Fun to Listen Together!

"Read the Scripture within 'the living Tradition of the whole Church.'"
CATECHISM OF THE CATHOLIC CHURCH, 113

"An authentic interpretation of the Bible must always be in harmony with the faith of the Catholic Church." **POPE BENEDICT XVI**

There is a difference between something that is *private* and something that is *personal*. Music is not usually a *private* affair. Musicians typically write music to share widely. They aspire to have it heard and appreciated. Occasionally, someone might write a *private* piece, something they keep to themselves, or that they share in only a limited fashion. Scripture is more like the former kind of music. It is God's love song, meant to be shared widely across centuries, continents, and cultures.

One danger in reading Scripture is to treat it as a *private* gift from God. When people do this, they disregard the interpretation that generations of Christians have shared with us. They disregard the teaching authority of the pope and bishops. They ignore the riches that many saints and holy women and men have found in the Scriptures through the ages. This treats Scripture as a *private* affair. It is dangerous because it separates a branch from the vine. It cuts one part of the body off from the others. It reinforces selfishness, ego, and individualism, which is the opposite of what the Spirit is accomplishing in the Church by creating unity in our diversity. Pope Benedict XVI reminded us, "One must *avoid the risk of an individualistic approach*, and remember that God's word is given to us precisely to build communion..."

Although Scripture isn't a *private* revelation to us, it is very *personal*. God wants to speak not just generically to the whole Church, but to each of us individually. As with any song, every listener finds a unique meaning because it resonates with our own life uniquely. A song means something *personal* to you because it was your prom song, or the song played at your grandfather's funeral, or the first song you sang in front of an audience. We all hear the same music, but we hear it *personally*.

So how do we avoid falling into the *private* trap? God's own solution is the Church, guided by the Holy Spirit we receive in Baptism and Confirmation. The Spirit is present in the community, in its sacramental life, and in its magisterium (which means the teaching authority of the pope and bishops). The Spirit is present in this community to guide our reading and to test our interpretations against the faith of the Church so that we stay true to the faith of the Apostles.

This is a big part of why Christians gather together on Sundays to hear the word of God. We read it alone at home too, but it is especially important to hear it proclaimed and interpreted in the faith community. Scripture, as I've said, is like a love song from God. And it's not unlike any other songs we listen to. On the one hand, we listen on our own, and we find *personal* meaning. But don't we also love to listen together with friends? Don't we love to hear other people's interpretations of the lyrics? Don't we love to learn the backstory? Don't we love to hear how a song has inspired others? Isn't it fun to listen together? Scripture is like that.

Praying with the Bible

1 INVITE THE HOLY SPIRIT

Come, O Holy Spirit, and help me to open the Bible with a readiness to hear God's word and a willingness to receive and share your gift of Wisdom in and with the Church. (*Pause in silence.*) (*Now read the passage…*)

> *Let no one despise your youth, but set the believers an example in speech and conduct, in love, in faith, in purity. Until I [St. Paul] arrive, give attention to the public reading of scripture, to exhorting, to teaching.* 1 TIMOTHY 4:12-13

2 TALK TO JESUS

Now, talk to Jesus as a friend, in your own words, from your heart. What part of St. Paul's advice to Timothy seems to carry God's word to you today? Ask Jesus about it. What does he desire of you? Will anyone despise you for it? What are your hopes and fears? Talk to Jesus about them.

3 GIVE GLORY TO THE FATHER

Make a decision about reading Scripture both alone and in the Church community. Can you set aside more time for it? Can you continue with good practices you have already established? Recognize that when we read Scripture prayerfully, inviting the Holy Spirit to enlighten us with Wisdom, we become closer to Christ, which is the glory of God the Father. The Father wants to bring us into the dynamic love that is perfect Unity and Trinity. As the Father and the Son are one in the Holy Spirit, so God the Father rejoices when the Spirit draws us into life with Christ, who alone brings us into the life of the Trinity! This is what we mean by salvation. This is what the love song we call Scripture is all about.

Confirmed in the Faith

QUESTIONS TO HELP US GROW STRONGER

Pick one or two questions to reflect on as you think about the meaning of your Confirmation and life in the Spirit.

- The word "confirmation" means being strengthened in faith. How can I allow the Spirit to continue to strengthen my faith through engagement with the Scriptures?

- Do I read the Bible on my own at all? Do I go to Mass to hear it read publicly and interpreted in light of the Catholic faith?

- The faith community includes many professionals who have studied the Bible a lot, including pastors, deacons, religious sisters and brothers, youth ministers, theology teachers, scholars, and religious education professionals, just to name a few. Why is it valuable to have this faith community as a check on my own understanding as I read the Bible?

- One of the Gifts of the Holy Spirit that we receive in Confirmation is Wisdom. How can I open that gift in order to experience the Bible *personally* as the word of God in my own life?

My Bible Journal

A SPACE FOR PERSONAL REFLECTIONS

_____

_____

"Moreover, we possess the prophetic message that is altogether reliable. You will do well to be attentive to it, as to a lamp shining in a dark place, until day dawns and the morning star rises in your hearts. Know this first of all, that there is no prophecy of scripture that is a matter of personal interpretation, for no prophecy ever came through human will; but rather human beings moved by the holy Spirit spoke under the influence of God." **2 PETER 1:19-21**

CHAPTER 4

A Symphony of Voices

"No single interpretation can exhaust the meaning of the whole, which is a symphony of many voices."

THE PONTIFICAL BIBLICAL COMMISSION

G et a bunch of friends together and start talking about music, and you'll find that there are a lot of different opinions. Who's the best singer? What's the greatest band ever? What does this or that song actually mean? Which version is the best? These kinds of questions don't usually lead to a single, undisputed answer. It's the nature of music that it carries a multitude of meanings and interpretations. It's part of the fun.

I like the idea that there is a "symphony of many voices" when interpreting the Bible too. It's a powerful musical metaphor that fits well with our sense of the Bible as God's love song. Very rarely can passages in the Bible be pinned down to just one meaning. After all, God is speaking to many, many people through these same verses. Just as with music, every person hears something different, something unique, something personal. And yet those personal meanings all fit together in the Church community or else we'd have a cacophony (noise) instead of a symphony.

Every Bible passage has a range of different meanings, such as a literal meaning, a spiritual meaning, a meaning based on symbols and metaphors, and a moral meaning. It often leads to many opinions and many different interpretations. That's okay! That's the "symphony of many voices." God's love song cannot be reduced to a monotone.

But... the fact that there are many opinions doesn't mean they are all correct or acceptable. Some things are simply wrong. For instance, if someone said that Elvis wrote "Uptown Funk," we can easily prove that is wrong. It's the same with the Bible. Sometimes an interpretation is just plain wrong or even dangerous. For example, Jesus said, "If your right eye causes you to sin, tear it out and throw it away. It is better for you to lose one of your members than to have your whole body thrown into Gehenna" (Matthew 5:29). If someone interpreted this literally and was thinking of doing harm to their own body, they are reading it wrong. Jesus was using hyperbole—an exaggeration—to express how serious it is to reject sin. He didn't mean to literally pluck our eyes out!

For the most part, though, the Church is very comfortable with the "symphony of many voices." Lots of Christians have opened the gifts of the Holy Spirit—especially Knowledge, Wisdom, and Understanding—to make sense of the Bible in their own lives. Pope Pius XII said we have the "true liberty of the children of God" to use our "skill and genius...[to] contribute...to the advantage of all." Only when an interpretation goes off track does the Church use its teaching authority to help guide us back to a Christian understanding. Most of the time, though, it's more like a great conversation among friends debating what a song means, or why it was written, or who sings it best. Get the right people together, and that type of conversation could go all night. It's part of the fun!

Praying with the Bible

1 INVITE THE HOLY SPIRIT

Come, O Holy Spirit, and help me not to be rigid, but to be open to the many meanings and interpretations of Scripture that are faithful to Christ. Help me to hear the Bible as a love song with a "symphony of many voices." (*Pause in silence.*) (*Now read the passage…*)

> *When the angels went away from them into heaven, the shepherds said to one another, "Let us go over to Bethlehem and see this thing that has happened, which the Lord has made known to us." And they went with haste and found Mary and Joseph, and the baby lying in a manger. And when they saw it, they made known the saying that had been told them concerning this child [that he will be the Savior]. And all who heard it wondered at what the shepherds told them. But Mary treasured up all these things, pondering them in her heart.* LUKE 2:15-19

2 TALK TO JESUS

Now, talk to Jesus as a friend, in your own words, from your heart. Imagine the setting of the Scripture passage you just read. What thoughts and feelings arise? What questions? How does it connect with your own life? Share your thoughts with Jesus.

3 GIVE GLORY TO THE FATHER

Recognizing and appreciating the "symphony of many voices" gives glory to the Father. It is the Father's love song after all. But sometimes it may not make sense to us. We may be overwhelmed by the message or by the multitude of interpreters, just as Joseph and the others "wondered at what the shepherds told them." Wonder is a good thing! Wonder and Awe is a gift of the Holy Spirit. The fact that God can speak a living word to every single person in history through this ancient text should fill us with Wonder and

Awe! Like Mary, we could "treasure up all these things" and ponder them in our hearts. This pondering is an expression of Wonder and Awe. It is one way we give glory to the Father.

Confirmed in the Faith

QUESTIONS TO HELP US GROW STRONGER

Pick one or two questions to reflect on as you think about the meaning of your Confirmation and life in the Spirit.

- Do you enjoy conversations with friends about music, even when you debate or disagree? If so, what makes those conversations fun?

- How does the fact that God can use the Bible to speak to every single person in history in a personal way fill you with Wonder and Awe at the mystery of God?

- Can you think of examples of parts of the Bible that have been interpreted badly over the years, causing harm and not being faithful to Christ's message of love?

My Bible Journal

A SPACE FOR PERSONAL REFLECTIONS

"Who is able to understand, Lord, all the richness of even one of your words? There is more that eludes us than we can understand. We are like the thirsty drinking from a fountain. Your word has as many aspects as the perspectives of those who study it." **ST. EPHREM**

CHAPTER 5

The Songwriter's Perspective

"The historical-critical method is the indispensable method for the scientific study of the meaning of ancient texts. Holy Scripture, inasmuch as it is the 'Word of God in human language,' has been composed by human authors in all its various parts and in all the sources that lie behind them. Because of this, its proper understanding not only admits the use of this method but actually requires it."

THE PONTIFICAL BIBLICAL COMMISSION

A famous song in the history of music is "Tears in Heaven" performed by Eric Clapton. The official music video has over 80 million views on YouTube. The song begins, "Would you know my name if I saw you in heaven? Would it be the same if I saw you in heaven?" Later, Clapton sings, "Beyond the door, there's peace I'm sure, and I know there'll be no more tears in heaven." It's a very slow, sad song. But what does it mean? What is it all about? To really understand the song, we need to know what Clapton was going through. It turns out, his four-year-old son, Conor, had recently died a tragic death by falling from a window. Clapton was deep in mourning. Music was his outlet for healing and hope. He yearned to see his little boy again someday in heaven.

You see how powerful knowing the backstory can be? I bet you can think of other examples from your favorite music. It's the same with the Bible. The writings are about two thousand years old or more, and they are frequently based on oral traditions that are even older. To understand them properly, we have to ask what the original writers meant. What was on their minds? What were they going through? What was happening in history at that time and place? What was the culture like?

The historical-critical method is the way biblical scholars figure out the backstory of the Bible. "Historical" means just what you'd think—trying to understand what was going on back then. "Critical" does not mean criticizing, however. It means using reason and critical thinking, just like you do in school. Catholic Scripture scholars use critical thinking about the history of the Bible to get at the backstory. Only then can we appreciate what the various parts of the Bible are meant to communicate. Without doing this work, we are in danger of reading it wrong. We are in danger of making an idol of the text itself! But the Bible is a love song from God. It is God we worship, not the text. And to understand the love song, we really do need to know what the writers had in mind. Our cultures and our history are very different from theirs, after all. The same words mean different things over the course of time and in different cultures. The Holy Spirit gives us Wisdom and Understanding to help us with this challenging work.

Praying with the Bible

1 INVITE THE HOLY SPIRIT

Come, O Holy Spirit, guide our Scripture scholars as they employ the gifts of Wisdom and Understanding to find the ancient meaning of biblical texts. Help me to learn from them, humbly acknowledging that, when it comes to the Bible, there is a backstory that gives more meaning than the words themselves reveal. (*Pause in silence.*) (*Now read the passage…*)

> *"You have heard that it was said to your ancestors, 'You shall not kill; and whoever kills will be liable to judgment.' But I say to you, whoever is angry with his brother will be liable to judgment…and whoever says, 'You fool,' will be liable to fiery Gehenna. Therefore, if you bring your gift to the altar, and there recall that your brother has anything against you, leave your gift there at the altar, go first and be reconciled with your brother, and then come and offer your gift."* MATTHEW 5:21-24

2 TALK TO JESUS

Now, talk to Jesus as a friend, in your own words, from your heart. Express to him any anger you have. Ask for his help in dealing with it in healthy ways. Pray for peace and reconciliation in families, in communities, and in the world.

3 GIVE GLORY TO THE FATHER

Pope Francis says that the name of God is Mercy. When we imitate God by acting mercifully, it gives the Father glory. In this passage from Matthew, Jesus calls us to the deeper meaning of the Scripture passage he quotes. It is not just murder that offends God, it is also the kind of anger that divides people and in the worst cases leads to murder and even genocide. Jesus showed us that perfect love leaves no room for this kind of anger. (Righteous anger is something altogether different. Jesus showed this kind of anger when he chased the money changers out of the temple). On the cross, Jesus did not express hate, vengeance, or destructive anger toward his torturers. Instead, he said, "Father, forgive them, they know not what they do" (Luke 23:34). How can I follow his example and give glory to the Father?

Confirmed in the Faith

QUESTIONS TO HELP US GROW STRONGER

Pick one or two questions to reflect on as you think about the meaning of your Confirmation and life in the Spirit.

- How does knowing the backstory help me to know the meaning of a song or a Bible passage better?

- How much do I know the backstory of the many books of the Bible? How could I learn more?

- Do I ever fall into the trap of reading the Bible literally instead of seeking the deeper meaning and listening for the living word of God speaking today?

- Why do you think the Catholic Church values its biblical scholars who are experts in ancient texts, languages, and cultures?

My Bible Journal

A SPACE FOR PERSONAL REFLECTIONS

_____

_____

"Without the work of the Spirit, there would always be a risk of remaining limited to the written text alone. This would open the way to a fundamentalist reading, which needs to be avoided, lest we betray the inspired, dynamic and spiritual character of the sacred text. As the Apostle reminds us: 'The letter kills, but the Spirit gives life' (2 Corinthians 3:6). The Holy Spirit, then, makes sacred Scripture the living word of God." **POPE FRANCIS**

CHAPTER 6

Did I Hear that Right??

"The Scripture is not in the reading, but in the understanding."

ST. HILARY OF POITIERS

Did you ever listen to a song and find out later that you heard the lyrics wrong? I still remember one year when a DJ had me laughing on my ride to work when she confessed that she thought Charlie Puth was singing, "You've been runnin' round...with that turtle on your knee," instead of, "You've been runnin' round...throwin' that dirt all on my name." Listen to it yourself. I can definitely hear what she heard! Has this ever happened to you with other songs?

Scripture is full of crazy things that make us say, "Did I hear that right?" Sometimes it's just that we misheard the reading, and it can be funny. For example, little kids often think Jesus said, "Our Father, who *aren't* in heaven" instead of "Who *art* in heaven!" Sometimes, though, the verse itself leaves us wondering. For instance, in Psalm 137 verse 9, the Bible says, "Blessed the one who seizes your children and smashes them against the rock." Did I hear that right? How can we call *that* the word of God?

We can't take all of Scripture literally. If we are going to read the Bible right, we need tools to understand it. After all, as St. Hilary noted above, it's the understanding that matters. We'll also need the presence of the Spirit to guide us. Understanding, after all, is one of the gifts of the Holy Spirit we receive in Confirmation.

Catholic Scripture scholars use a tool called *hermeneutics* (pronounced: herma-noodix). That's just a fancy term that refers to theories and methods (the "rules and tools") of interpreting. I like the term because it comes from the name of the Greek messenger god, Hermes. *Hermeneutics* helps us to understand the message! My favorite guide for this process is St. Augustine. As a young man, he left the Catholic faith, much to the chagrin of his mother, St. Monica, who never stopped praying for his return. One stumbling block for him was the Bible. However, after he met St. Ambrose, the bishop of Milan, he converted back to the Catholic faith. Monica's prayers were answered. Ambrose had taught Augustine how to read the Bible properly. In turn, Augustine handed on some key advice. It can be summarized in two rules:

> **Rule 1:** Since the Great Commandment is to love God above all things and to love our neighbor as ourselves, the word of God cannot contradict this. In other words, all of Scripture should lead us to a greater love of God, neighbor, and self. If it doesn't, then we are surely reading it wrong.

> **Rule 2:** Anytime it seems that God or a hero is engaging in something sinful or promoting something evil, the passage should be read symbolically for its spiritual meaning.

This is where the historical-critical method that we learned in the last chapter comes in handy. Scripture scholars tell us that Psalm 137 was written when Jerusalem had been sacked by the Babylonians, who also destroyed their sacred temple and took the Jews to Babylon as captives. The writer was expressing a Jewish desire to completely destroy their enemies. But certainly, God is not encouraging us to bash babies' heads on rocks in order to be blessed. St. Augustine teaches us to read this symbolically. Psalms are songs, and like any songs, they use metaphors. In this case, we can read the warfare passages as metaphors for our battle against sin and evil, which is exactly what the early Church father Origen did. It is difficult to do battle with sins that have grown to full maturity in our lives, becoming habits and having a lot of power over us. Instead, we should destroy them while they are still "children." A literalist reading would have us committing or condoning murder. But going deeper, we find the spiritual meaning, and in so doing, we can hear the living word of God speaking to us today about destroying our sins.

Praying with the Bible

1 INVITE THE HOLY SPIRIT

Come, O Holy Spirit, and help me to recognize that love is the greatest commandment and the key to understanding the Bible. Help me to see honestly and humbly whom I am not loving. *(Pause in silence.) (Now read the passage...)*

> *A scholar of the law tested [Jesus] by asking, "Teacher, which commandment in the law is the greatest?" He said to him, "You shall love the Lord, your God, with all your heart, with all your soul, and with all your mind. This is the greatest and the first commandment. The second is like it: You shall love your neighbor as yourself. The whole law and the prophets depend on these two commandments."* **MATTHEW 22:35-40**

2 TALK TO JESUS

Talk to Jesus as a friend, in your own words, and from your heart. Talk about your ability to love. Ask for the grace to grow in love of God, neighbor, and self. Ask him for patience and forgiveness when you fall short. Trust in your friend Jesus' love for you.

3 GIVE GLORY TO THE FATHER

Make a decision to keep doing something that is leading you to greater love, or to change something where your love is lacking, so that you grow closer to loving God with all your heart, soul, and mind. This will give great glory to God the Father, who desires love above all.

Confirmed in the Faith

QUESTIONS TO HELP US GROW STRONGER

Pick one or two questions to reflect on as you think about the meaning of your Confirmation and life in the Spirit.

- Do I know of any times people have read the Bible in a way that didn't lead to greater love of God, neighbor, and self? Have I done so?

- Is there anyone I can help by teaching them, just as St. Ambrose taught St. Augustine?

- Is there anyone who is straying from faith in God, for whom I can pray, as St. Monica prayed for her son?

- What is the biggest challenge in today's world for living out the Great Commandment?

My Bible Journal

A SPACE FOR PERSONAL REFLECTIONS

"Interpretation of the inspired Scripture must be attentive above all to what God wants to reveal through the sacred authors for our salvation. What comes from the Spirit is not fully 'understood except by the Spirit's action.'"
CATECHISM OF THE CATHOLIC CHURCH, 137
(QUOTING ORIGEN, ONE OF THE EARLY FATHERS OF THE CHURCH)

CHAPTER 7

What Kind of Music Is This?

"Clearly to be rejected...is every attempt at [applying the Bible in a way that is]... contrary to...justice and charity, such as...the use of the Bible to justify racial segregation, anti-Semitism, or sexism..." **THE PONTIFICAL BIBLICAL COMMISSION**

A friend of mine from Iraq was playing Arabic music in his car one day as we headed to lunch together. It was really interesting because it's not music that I ever listen to on my own. I don't understand much of the language or the culture. I couldn't even tell what the music was about. If he weren't there to interpret it for me, I would have been lost.

We can feel lost with the Bible too. A lot of things in the Bible just don't make sense in our world today because it was written in languages and cultures different from ours. For example, there is a love song in the Bible called the Song of Songs. In it, the lover describes the beauty of the woman he loves. But here's where it gets weird. He says to her, "Your hair is like a flock of goats streaming down Mount Gilead. Your teeth are like a flock of ewes to be shorn, that come up from the washing..." (Song of Songs 4:1–2). If I hadn't told you this was an ancient love song, would you have known? To interpret the Bible wisely we have to consider the culture, the genre, and the context of each book and passage we read.

Culture. Just like with my friend's Arabic music, we need translators and interpreters to understand the meaning of things from cultures we aren't familiar with. For Catholics, we turn to our Biblical scholars. In the case of the Song of Songs, it might just be funny to read the ancient descriptions. But in some cases, the cultural differences can lead to violence and oppression. For example, St. Paul wrote, "Slaves, obey your earthly masters with respect and fear...just as you would obey Christ" (Ephesians 6:5). Slaveholders have used this to justify slavery. They misinterpreted the Bible! They read it literally as if God had dictated these words instead of recognizing that some of what St. Paul wrote was the cultural baggage of his day. Remember, the Bible is the word of God expressed in human language.

Genre. How we read something depends on what type of writing it is. We read poems differently from comic books. We read news articles differently from science fiction or romance novels. Once we know what we're reading, we know how to read it. Different books in the Bible have different genres. Knowing that the Song of Songs is a love song, full of imagery and passion, helps us to read it correctly. We realize that it is in the Bible as a metaphor for God's love. Reading it literally would be silly. Whose hair is actually like a flock of goats?

Context. One of the most important rules for reading the Bible is this: Don't read things out of context. For example, the defenders of slavery were pulling verses out of the Bible out of context. When we look at the whole Bible, we see that the major story of the entire Old Testament is that God sent Moses to free the Hebrews from slavery in Egypt. The Bible makes it clear that God not only doesn't support slavery but actually works against it. God wants us to be free! In the words of Scripture scholar Walter Brueggemann, "God is the freedom-giver." You'd never guess that, though, if you read that verse from St. Paul out of context.

Praying with the Bible

1 INVITE THE HOLY SPIRIT

Come, O Holy Spirit, and grant me the gift of Courage to stand up for justice and peace, as the prophets did in the Bible and as holy women and men do to this day. Help me to reject any reading of Scripture that promotes division, dehumanization, and destruction of human life and dignity. (*Pause in silence.*) (*Now read the passage…*)

> There is neither Jew nor Greek, there is neither slave nor free person, there is not male and female; for you are all one in Christ Jesus. GALATIANS 3:25-28

2 TALK TO JESUS

Now, talk to Jesus as a friend, in your own words, from your heart. Have you ever witnessed the Bible used to deny people their God-given dignity? Have you witnessed the Bible used to make it seem that some people are better than others? Tell Jesus about any bigotry and prejudice you've witnessed or experienced. Ask for his strength and guidance to promote unity and peace.

3 GIVE GLORY TO THE FATHER

St. Augustine reminded us that the whole Bible has a message of love for God, our neighbor, and ourselves. If we interpret it otherwise, then not only have we read it wrong, we have not glorified the Father. "The glory of God is the human person fully alive," said St. Irenaeus. We fail to glorify the Father if we use the Bible to diminish the life of others through slavery, sexism, homophobia, anti-Semitism, racism, or any other lack of love. Make a commitment to read the Bible in a fully "pro-life" manner. After all, in the inspired words of St. Paul, "Love does no harm to a neighbor; therefore, love is the fulfillment of the law" (Romans 13:10).

Confirmed in the Faith

QUESTIONS TO HELP US GROW STRONGER

Pick one or two questions to reflect on as you think about the meaning of your Confirmation and life in the Spirit.

- Why do you think it's important to know something about the culture that each writer of the Bible was part of?

- Why do you think knowing the genre of a particular book in the Bible is important for getting an accurate interpretation of the meaning?

- "Proof-texting" is when someone pulls a quote from the Bible out of context, usually just to prove a point. Why do you think the Catholic Church is against this practice?

My Bible Journal

A SPACE FOR PERSONAL REFLECTIONS

_____

_____

_____

_____

_____

_____

"All the evil in the world is derived from not knowing clearly the truths of Sacred Scripture." **ST. TERESA OF AVILA**

CHAPTER 8

This Song Means So Much to Me! You Have No Idea!

"Devotion to the word of God is not simply one of many devotions, beautiful but somewhat optional. It goes to the very heart and identity of Christian life. The word has the power to transform lives."

CONFERENCE OF THE CATHOLIC BISHOPS OF INDIA

Randy Travis is a country singer who had a very popular love song called "Forever and Ever, Amen" (over 45 million views on YouTube). The song reached number 1 on the country music charts and was certified gold. It became a popular wedding song as well, since its theme was love that would last "forever and ever." In 2018, thirty years after the song won a Grammy, a writer called it a "classic country song that has stood the test of time."

For one little girl, though, this song meant a lot more than it did for most other people. It meant so much to her that her family wrote a letter to Randy Travis. You see, the song includes the lyrics, "They say time takes its toll on a body, makes a young girl with brown hair turn gray; but honey I don't care, I ain't in love with your hair. And if it all fell out, well I'd love you anyway." For almost everyone else, these lines were about loving someone even as they grow old. But for this young girl it was different. She had cancer and had lost all of her hair during chemotherapy.

She was too embarrassed to go outside and play with her friends until she heard this song. It convinced her she was still loved and lovable. She wasn't ashamed anymore. The song changed her life.

If a song can have that much meaning on a personal level, imagine how much God's love song can reach us and change our lives. In fact, we should expect it. If we have "ears to hear" as Jesus wanted us to have (see Matthew 11:15), we will hear the same stories that everyone hears, but we will also hear God speaking to us personally. St. Augustine put it this way: "When you read the Bible, God speaks to you; when you pray, you speak to God."

Over the centuries, saints have heard the word of God speaking to them from the pages of the Bible. Saint Francis of Assisi heard God's call from the Bible to live without riches as Christ did, and "exulting in the Holy Spirit, [he] immediately cried out: 'This is what I want, this is what I ask for, this I long to do with all my heart!'" Saint Thérèse of the Child Jesus said, "No sooner do I glance at the gospel, but immediately I breathe in the fragrance of the life of Jesus and I know where to run." God is calling every one of us to holiness. We are all meant to be saints. Saints are those who hear the love song of God wooing them and choose to respond to God's love with love. Their lives are the proof. They are filled with love and mercy, expressed in prayer and in service, with a willingness to sacrifice just as Christ did.

St. Augustine tells us that to hear the Bible this way, we need to approach the Scriptures with Reverence, which is acting with a sense of God's presence. St. Augustine says Reverence is present when we turn from sin and recognize that God's word "is better and truer than anything we could devise by our own wisdom." Fortunately for us, Reverence is one of the gifts of the Holy Spirit we receive in Confirmation. If we use that gift, we'll find that the Bible has more meaning for us than we had ever imagined. It will change our life!

Praying with the Bible

1 INVITE THE HOLY SPIRIT

Come, O Holy Spirit, and grant me the gift of Reverence, that I may recognize that God is speaking through the Bible, and help me to act accordingly. *(Pause in silence.) (Now read the passage…)*

> *The tempter…said to [Jesus], "If you are the Son of God, command that these stones become loaves of bread." He said in reply, "It is written: One does not live by bread alone, but by every word that comes forth from the mouth of God." Then the devil…made him stand on the parapet of the temple, and said to him, "If you are the Son of God, throw yourself down. For it is written: He will command his angels concerning you and with their hands they will support you, lest you dash your foot against a stone." Jesus answered him, "Again it is written, You shall not put the Lord, your God, to the test." Then the devil took him up to a very high mountain, and showed him all the kingdoms of the world in their magnificence, and he said to him, "All these I shall give to you, if you will prostrate yourself and worship me." At this, Jesus said to him, "Get away, Satan! It is written: The Lord, your God, shall you worship, and him alone shall you serve."* MATTHEW 4:3-10

2 TALK TO JESUS

Now, talk to Jesus as a friend, in your own words, from your heart. What temptations are bothering you? Ask Jesus for help in overcoming them.

3 GIVE GLORY TO THE FATHER

When we recognize God's presence, we see the sacredness in people, things, places, and events. We act with Reverence. Jesus recognized God's presence in Scripture; the devil did not. Notice how differently they treat the Bible. Choose to follow Jesus' example of Reverence, and in so doing give glory to the Father.

Confirmed in the Faith

QUESTIONS TO HELP US GROW STRONGER

Pick one or two questions to reflect on as you think about the meaning of your Confirmation and life in the Spirit.

- Both Jesus and the devil quoted the Bible. What was the difference?

- How can I show more Reverence in my life, respecting God's presence in all of creation, in all people, in the Scriptures, and in the sacraments, especially the Eucharist?

- Why do you think Reverence is so important to reading the Bible?

- If the Bible is the same text for everyone, how can it possibly be personal?

My Bible Journal

A SPACE FOR PERSONAL REFLECTIONS

_____

_____

_____

_____

"If today you hear his voice, harden not your hearts."
RESPONSE TO PSALM 95, SUNDAY LECTIONARY

"The most profound interpretation of Scripture comes precisely from those who let themselves be shaped by the word of God through listening, reading, and assiduous meditation."
POPE BENEDICT XVI

Part II

SINGING *a* LOVE SONG BACK *to* GOD

"In its pages his image stands out, living and breathing; diffusing everywhere around consolation in trouble, encouragement to virtue and attraction to the love of God." **POPE LEO XIII**

"Having received the beautiful gift of God's word, we embrace it 'in much affliction, with joy inspired by the Holy Spirit' (1 Thessalonians 1:6)....The prophets proclaimed the times of Jesus, in which we now live, as a revelation of joy. 'Shout and sing for joy!' (Isaiah 12:6)."
POPE FRANCIS

CHAPTER 9

Singing a Love Song Back to God

"[The]...ongoing dialogue with the [Bible] about its subject matter...
must be pursued with relentless love by those who believe that this text,
thoroughly human as Jesus himself, is yet a privileged mediator
of the encounter between God and humanity." **SANDRA SCHNEIDERS**

S r. Sandra Schneiders, IHM, is a religious sister and a theologian in the Catholic Church. In her quote above (from her book *The Revelatory Text*), she reminds us that the Bible is a special way in which we encounter God. She reminds us that the Bible is like Jesus, human and divine. The human aspect is always present and is sometimes disturbing, such as when the author of Psalm 137 said that the person who bashed the children's heads against the rocks would be blessed (see chapter 6). The divine aspect is the encounter with the living God, speaking to us personally and as a Church today. That encounter is always focused on the same thing: God revealing Godself as "nothing but mercy and love" (as St. Thérèse said) and singing a love song to us. Schneiders indicates that a response is needed. The only faithful response to a love so strong is our own "relentless love."

Love songs are not always happy. They are not always "Forever and Ever, Amen." Sometimes a love song is about unrequited love and the heartache that goes with the rejection. Anyone who has ever been rejected knows that it is a terrible feeling. Anyone who has ever gone through a breakup knows it can be painful. What we recognize above all is that love must be a two-way street. Love cannot be forced. It must be free and mutual.

The same is true of God's love. Catherine Maresca says, "There is no need for coercion, forced conversions, or threats of hell." God leaves us free to respond to love, but never stops wooing us in this life. When we sense this wooing, we may be filled with Wonder and Awe. The Holy Spirit helps us to recognize the pure beauty of what God is and what God is offering. Sofia Cavalletti puts it this way: "The nature of wonder is not a force that pushes us passively from behind; it is situated ahead of us and attracts us with irresistible force....It makes us advance toward it, filled with enchantment." Have you ever felt that? Have you ever felt God's presence in a new baby, a sunset, a beautiful landscape, a church, a pet, or someone or something else? Did it just fill you with Wonder and Awe? Cavalletti's point is that God doesn't need to force us. When we sense God's love, goodness, truth, and beauty, we are simply drawn to it. It is irresistible! It's very similar to how we fall in love. Nobody forces us to love them. That wouldn't be love. Instead, we are drawn to their beauty and goodness.

For those who hear the word of God and are drawn to God irresistibly, the natural response is to sing a love song in return. We call this worship. It's why Catholics go to Mass. Cardinal Ratzinger, who later became Pope Benedict XVI, said, "The pure relationship of love...[that] is what worship is supposed to be." We hear the readings at Mass, not as dead ancient letters, but as God speaking to us now, expressing love and inviting us into the life of Love itself, which is the Trinity! By receiving Jesus in the Eucharist at Holy Communion, we are joined to Jesus in his perfect offering of love to the Father.

Praying with the Bible

1 INVITE THE HOLY SPIRIT

Come, O Holy Spirit. Fill me with Wonder and Awe in God's presence so that I might be drawn irresistibly forward into the life of the Trinity, which is Love itself. (*Pause in silence.*) (*Now read the passage…*)

> *Beloved, let us love one another, because love is of God; everyone who loves is begotten by God and knows God. Whoever is without love does not know God, for God is love. In this way the love of God was revealed to us: God sent his only Son into the world so that we might have life through him…. No one has ever seen God. Yet, if we love one another, God remains in us, and his love is brought to perfection in us. This is how we know that we remain in him and he in us, that he has given us of his Spirit. Moreover, we have seen and testify that the Father sent his Son as savior of the world… We have come to know and to believe in the love God has for us. God is love, and whoever remains in love remains in God and God in him [or her]. In this is love brought to perfection among us, that we have confidence on the day of judgment because as he is, so are we in this world. There is no fear in love, but perfect love drives out fear because fear has to do with punishment, and so one who fears is not yet perfect in love. We love because he first loved us. If anyone says, "I love God," but hates his brother [or sister], he is a liar; for whoever does not love a brother [or sister] whom he has seen cannot love God whom he has not seen. This is the commandment we have from him: whoever loves God must also love his brother [and his sister].* 1 JOHN 4:7-21

2 TALK TO JESUS

Now, talk to Jesus as a friend, in your own words, from your heart. What fears keep you from trusting God's love for you? Does your love for God show in your love for other people?

3 GIVE GLORY TO THE FATHER

Make a commitment to put love first in your life, as Jesus did, for the glory of the Father. Are you wondering what love means? For Christians, it is never just a feeling. Love is active. It is unselfish. It serves others, especially those most in need. Love wants everyone to experience the fullness of life and is willing to sacrifice for them. This love is sometimes called *agape*.

Confirmed in the Faith

QUESTIONS TO HELP US GROW STRONGER

Pick one or two questions to reflect on as you think about the meaning of your Confirmation and life in the Spirit.

- Have I ever thought about worship as an act of love?

- What do you think John meant when he said we are liars if we say we love God but don't love one another?

- If Scripture is God's love song to me, how can I sing my love back to God?

- One of the gifts of the Holy Spirit is Good Judgment. Is there any decision in life where we need Good Judgment more than the decision about whether and how to respond to God's love? Why is this decision so important?

My Bible Journal

A SPACE FOR PERSONAL REFLECTIONS

_____

_____

_____

"The word of the Lord. Do I love the word of God? Do I live by it? Do I serve it willingly? Help me, Lord, to live by your word." **POPE SAINT JOHN PAUL II**

CHAPTER 10

Singing All Day Long!

"Thro' all the tumult and the strife
I hear the music ringing;
It finds an echo in my soul—
How can I keep from singing?"

"HOW CAN I KEEP FROM SINGING," TRADITIONAL HYMN

Imagine if someone you love wrote a love song for you. Or a love letter. Wouldn't you listen or read it again and again? Most people would. We linger over the words and the feelings. We savor the message and the meaning. Most of all, we are filled with pure delight because the person we love also loves us! If it hasn't happened to you yet, it will. And all of your waiting will be worth it!

In a love song, it's not the words alone that are meaningful—it's also who wrote them. The literal words would mean nothing if they weren't backed by genuine feelings. The reason we keep reading a love letter or listening to a love song is because they remind us of someone we love. If you wrote back, wouldn't it thrill you if the other person treasured it? It proves they love you too! It means the feelings are mutual. It means they appreciate what you put into words or to music. It means they appreciate you and your love.

This is a good metaphor for the Bible. Scripture is like God's love song to the world. How do we receive that love song? Do we set it aside and not really bother with it? Imagine how terrible that would make you feel if you wrote a love song for someone. God doesn't have feelings the way we do—God is God, after all, not changeable like a human being. God is and forever remains perfect and unchanging love itself. Still, since God is expressing a desire for us to be swept up in this life of perfect love, we probably should not just set the love song aside. If we love God, we'll want to listen to it again and again.

In the Catholic tradition, there is an ancient form of prayer that is similar to how we react to a love song or a love letter. It is called the Liturgy of the Hours or the Divine Office. Monks and nuns for hundreds of years have been praying this way. Just as we would listen to a love song again and again, so too the Liturgy of the Hours involves coming back to the Bible multiple times a day. In between work, meals, recreation, and sleep, monks and nuns (and others) sanctify the day, symbolically, at all hours. In reality, they come together five times a day at least: 1) The Office of Readings (Vigils or Matins) prayed in the middle of the night, 2) Morning Prayer (Lauds), 3) Daytime Prayer (Terce/Sext/None), 4) Evening Prayer (Vespers), and 5) Night Prayer (Compline). You can find them on the iBreviary app and in other places.

You may have a special calling to be a monk or a nun, but most of us are called by God to different ways of life. Still, we know that there are monks and nuns all over the world who are praying at all hours of the day for us and on our behalf. The Holy Spirit unites us in prayer, forming us into the Communion of Saints. We can join them in their prayers at a monastery or on our own. We don't have to pray every section, but maybe just Morning Prayer and Evening Prayer, or maybe Night Prayer before bed. In any case, by coming back to the Bible every day, we show God that we are delighted with this love song! We just can't stop listening to it!

Praying with the Bible

■ INVITE THE HOLY SPIRIT

Come, O Holy Spirit. Grant me the gifts of Good Judgment and Reverence so that I might respond to God's love song in a way that demonstrates appreciation and love. (*Pause in silence.*) (*Now read the passage…*)

> *Watch carefully then how you live, not as foolish persons but as wise, making the most of the opportunity, because the days are evil. Therefore, do not continue in ignorance, but try to understand what is the will of the Lord. And do not get drunk on wine, in which lies debauchery, but be filled with the Spirit, addressing one another [in] psalms and hymns and spiritual songs, singing and playing to the Lord in your hearts, giving thanks always and for everything in the name of our Lord Jesus Christ to God the Father.*
> **EPHESIANS 5:15-20**

■ TALK TO JESUS

Now, talk to Jesus as a friend, in your own words, from your heart. Talk to him about whether "the days are evil" still, and ask for the Spirit's gift of Wisdom. Talk to him about the good in the world too, and how you can make "the most of the opportunity."

■ GIVE GLORY TO THE FATHER

St. Paul wrote the words above to the Church located in Ephesus (in modern-day Turkey). Many Christians believe that is where Mary spent her last days with the Apostle John. She is a perfect example of giving glory to the Father by "giving thanks always and for everything in the name of our Lord Jesus Christ." Have you expressed thanks to God? Meister Eckhart, writing in the Middle Ages, said, "If the only prayer you ever say in your entire life is thank you, it will be enough." In fact, "Eucharist" means "To give thanks." It is that important!

Confirmed in the Faith

QUESTIONS TO HELP US GROW STRONGER

Pick one or two questions to reflect on as you think about the meaning of your Confirmation and life in the Spirit.

- How would you react to someone you love writing a love song for you?

- Why do you think people save love letters and read them over and over again?

- Why do you think the Liturgy of the Hours has lasted for centuries?

- Do you ever think of the Bible as God's love song and keep listening to it again and again?

My Bible Journal

A SPACE FOR PERSONAL REFLECTIONS

"Among the forms of prayer which emphasize Sacred Scripture, the Liturgy of the Hours has an undoubted place. The Synod Fathers [that is, the bishops gathered together in council] called it 'a privileged form of hearing the word of God, inasmuch as it brings the faithful into contact with Scripture and the living Tradition of the Church.'" **POPE BENEDICT XVI**

CHAPTER 11

Mary's Song

"There, too, I listen on my knees, great Queen of all the Angels!
To that sweet canticle* that flows in rapture from thy soul;
so dost thou teach me how to sing like heavenly, glad evangels.*
And glorify my Jesus, Who alone can make me whole."

ST. THÉRÈSE OF LISIEUX

*a canticle is a song; evangels are those who proclaim the Good News

In the last chapter, I said that Mary was a great role model for always giving thanks to the Father. St. Thérèse put it this way: "O, how I love the Blessed Virgin….She is described as unapproachable, whereas she should be pointed to as a model. She is more of a Mother than a Queen." Mary is the perfect example of what we've been discussing. When we hear God's word, God's love song to us, we can't just ignore it. Not if God's love means something to us. We listen to the love song again and again, cherishing God's love for us. And if our love is real, we feel irresistibly drawn to respond by worshiping together at Mass, serving those in need, working for justice and peace, turning away from sin, and taking time to pray.

When Mary heard the word of God, it was through the angel Gabriel telling her God's plan to make her the mother of the Savior. She wasn't forced. Love never forces. Instead, she heard a love song and was free to respond. Mary replied, "Behold, I am the handmaid of the Lord. May it be done to me according to your word" (Luke 1:37). Then she visited her cousin Elizabeth, who was also miraculously pregnant (with John the

Baptist). Elizabeth said, "Most blessed are you among women, and blessed is the fruit of your womb. And how does this happen to me, that the mother of my Lord should come to me? For at the moment the sound of your greeting reached my ears, the infant in my womb leaped for joy. Blessed are you who believed that what was spoken to you by the Lord would be fulfilled" (Luke 1:42–45). Rather than take the praise for herself, Mary gave thanks and praise to God. Love is like that. When we are in love, we think not of ourselves but of the one we love. Mary's reply is the song called the "Magnificat" (about which St. Thérèse wrote the poetic lines above):

> "My soul proclaims the greatness of the Lord;
> my spirit rejoices in God my savior.
> For he has looked upon his handmaid's lowliness;
> behold, from now on will all ages call me blessed.
> The Mighty One has done great things for me,
> and holy is his name.
> His mercy is from age to age..."

Read the rest in Luke 1:46–55. As a good mother and model of faith, Mary teaches us that when we hear God's love song, we should sing right back. It is the call-and-response of love!

Praying with the Bible

1 INVITE THE HOLY SPIRIT

Come, O Holy Spirit. Fill my heart with song, that my life may be a response of love to the God who loves me so deeply. *(Pause in silence.) (Now read the passage…)*

> *Each year his parents went to Jerusalem for the feast of Passover, and when he was twelve years old, they went up according to festival custom… [A]s they were returning, the boy Jesus remained behind in Jerusalem, but his parents did not know it… After three days they found him in the temple, sitting in the midst of the teachers, listening to them and asking them questions, and all who heard him were astounded at his understanding and his answers. When his parents saw him, they were astonished, and his mother said to him, "Son, why have you done this to us? Your father and I have been looking for you with great anxiety." And he said to them, "Why were you looking for me? Did you not know that I must be about my Father's work?" But they did not understand what he said to them. He went down with them and came to Nazareth, and was obedient to them; and his mother kept all these things in her heart.* LUKE 2:41-51

2 TALK TO JESUS

Now, talk to Jesus as a friend, in your own words, from your heart. Have you ever felt like you lost Jesus? Like he was missing? Talk to him about it. Ask, as Mary and Joseph did, "Why have you done this to us?" As long as we keep talking together in prayer, the relationship continues.

3 GIVE GLORY TO THE FATHER

There is a line in the novel *A River Runs Through It* (made into a movie with Brad Pitt) that says: "We can love completely without complete understanding." This describes Mary in the scene above. Mary and Joseph didn't understand Jesus' excuse: "I must be about my Father's work." But even without complete understanding, there was total love. Mary "kept all these things in her heart." This is how we can glorify the Father too. Like Jesus, we should be about the Father's business. Like Mary, we should keep all of Jesus' words and actions in our hearts.

Confirmed in the Faith

QUESTIONS TO HELP US GROW STRONGER

Pick one or two questions to reflect on as you think about the meaning of your Confirmation and life in the Spirit.

- Mary used song to praise God. What gifts do you have that could be used to praise God?

- Jesus said he had to be about his Father's work. Is there any way for you to share in the Father's work too?

- St. Thérèse considered Mary a mother and a role model. How is she a mother and a model to Christians today? What about to you personally?

My Bible Journal

A SPACE FOR PERSONAL REFLECTIONS

_____

_____

_____

"The Church 'becomes herself a mother by accepting God's word with fidelity.' Like Mary, who first believed by accepting the word of God revealed to her at the Annunciation and by remaining faithful to that word in all her trials even unto the Cross, so too the Church becomes a mother when, accepting with fidelity the word of God, 'by her preaching and by baptism she brings forth to a new and immortal life children who are conceived of the Holy Spirit and born of God.'"

POPE ST. JOHN PAUL II

CHAPTER 12

Keeping All These Things in Our Hearts

"Ignorance of Scripture is ignorance of Christ."

ST. JEROME

The word of God is like a love song from God that we treasure in our hearts. In the last chapter, we saw that "Mary kept all these things" about Jesus "in her heart." In the Catholic tradition, an ancient and wonderful way of keeping these things in our hearts is called *lectio divina*, which is Latin for "divine reading." *Lectio divina* usually begins with an opening prayer asking for the gifts of the Holy Spirit. Then there are five stages of reading and prayer, described below (with the traditional Latin names in parentheses):

Opening Prayer, option 1: "Loving Master, shine the pure light of your divine knowledge in our hearts. Open the eyes of our minds that we may understand the message of your gospel. Instill in us reverence for your blessed commandments, that having conquered our sinful desires, we may pursue a spiritual life, thinking and doing all those things that are pleasing to you. For you, O Christ our God, are the light of our souls and bodies and to you do we offer glory, together with your Father who is without beginning and your all-holy, good, and life-giving Spirit now and forever and to the ages of ages. Amen." (Liturgy of St. John Chrysostom).

Opening Prayer, option 2: "Come, Holy Spirit, fill the hearts of your faithful people, and kindle in them the fire of your love.

> V. Send forth your spirit and they shall be created.
> R. And you shall renew the face of the earth.

Let us Pray. O God, you instructed the hearts of the faithful by the light of the Holy Spirit: grant that in the same Spirit we may be truly wise, and ever rejoice in the Spirit's consolation. Through Christ our Lord. Amen." (Roman Missal)

1. Reading (Lectio). Read the text slowly, trying to take in all the details. A good way to choose what part of the Bible to read is to use the same readings that Catholics (and others) around the world are reading. You can find the daily readings on the iBreviary app or from the U.S. Bishops' home page (USCCB.org; just click on the daily reading box).

2. Meditation (Meditatio). Now savor the text. Dwell on words or verses that struck you. Imagine yourself in the scene. Think about what this Bible passage means. Don't fall into the trap of literalism; instead, interpret the passage in light of Christ and the message of God's love.

3. Prayer (Oratio). Express to God whatever is on your mind from this reading. Let your heart speak to God's heart.

4. Contemplation (Contemplatio). Sit silently and allow God's silent voice to penetrate your soul. Trust that God is present and is speaking. Listen with the "ear of your heart," as St. Benedict said.

5. Action (Actio). As you end your *lectio divina* prayer, make a decision about your life as a follower of Christ. Has this reading inspired you to change in any way? Has it convinced you to stay strong in other commitments? Is it leading you to study more about the passage you read? Is it calling you to be less self-centered and to serve others more willingly? Pope Benedict XVI said, "We do well...to remember that the process of *lectio divina* is not concluded until it arrives at action (*actio*), which moves the believer to make his or her life a gift for others in charity."

Praying with the Bible

INVITE THE HOLY SPIRIT

In this chapter, let's practice praying *lectio divina*. Turn back to the beginning of the chapter and pray one of the opening prayers, asking for the gifts of the Holy Spirit. Then follow along the five stages:

1 **READING** *(Lectio)*

> *"You have heard that it was said, 'An eye for an eye and a tooth for a tooth.' But I say to you, offer no resistance to one who is evil. When someone strikes you on [your] right cheek, turn the other one to him as well. If anyone wants to go to law with you over your tunic, hand him your cloak as well. Should anyone press you into service for one mile, go with him for two miles. Give to the one who asks of you, and do not turn your back on one who wants to borrow. You have heard that it was said, 'You shall love your neighbor and hate your enemy.' But I say to you, love your enemies, and pray for those who persecute you, that you may be children of your heavenly Father, for he makes his sun rise on the bad and the good, and causes rain to fall on the just and the unjust. For if you love those who love you, what recompense will you have?"*
>
> **MATTHEW 5:38-46**

2 **MEDITATION** *(Meditatio)*

Look at the previous page for how to meditate on a passage.

3 **PRAYER** *(Oratio)*

Now, let your heart speak to God's heart. Pray in your own words.

4 **CONTEMPLATION** *(Contemplatio)*

Sit in silence for a few minutes. Quiet your mind. Listen with the "ear of your heart" for what God is speaking now, to you.

5 ACTION *(Actio)*

Make a decision that will help you to grow as a follower of Christ, remembering the words of St. James: "Be doers of the word and not hearers only, deluding yourselves" (James 1:22). Or as another translation puts it, "Act on this word. If all you do is listen to it, you are deceiving yourselves."

Confirmed in the Faith

QUESTIONS TO HELP US GROW STRONGER

Pick one or two questions to reflect on as you think about the meaning of your Confirmation and life in the Spirit.

- Why do you think we pray to the Holy Spirit before reading the Bible?

- Do you think *lectio divina* could be a helpful part of living out the commitment to Christ and the Church that you make in Confirmation?

- When we are in doubt about the meaning of a passage, where could we turn for help so that we avoid getting fundamentalist, misleading, or erroneous answers online?

My Bible Journal

A SPACE FOR PERSONAL REFLECTIONS

_____

_____

_____

_____

"Lectio divina...is truly 'capable of opening up to the faithful the treasures of God's word, but also of bringing about an encounter with Christ, the living word of God.'" **POPE BENEDICT XVI**

CHAPTER 13

Putting the Love Song to Music

"Whoever sings, prays twice." **CATECHISM OF THE CATHOLIC CHURCH (CCC), 1156 (QUOTE OFTEN ATTRIBUTED TO ST. AUGUSTINE)**

"In the song of the lover, there is love." **ST. AUGUSTINE**

Mary, as we saw, responded to the word of God by singing. As a Jew, this tradition of turning to God in song was deep in her heart. The Jewish Scriptures (which Christians call the Old Testament) shaped her faith in God, and they are full of music. We already talked about the love song called the Song of Songs. There are also the Psalms, which Jews and Christians sing in their worship services to this day. Also, there is the song that the Israelites sang to glorify God for freeing them from slavery: "I will sing to the Lord, for he is gloriously triumphant....In your love you led the people you redeemed; in your strength you guided them to your holy dwelling" (Exodus 15:1,13). Christians sing this song every year at the Easter Vigil to remember that just as God freed the Chosen People from slavery, so too Christ delivers us from sin and death.

In the second part of the Christian Bible (the New Testament), we find songs as well, including a reference to Jesus singing a hymn with his disciples at the Last Supper (Mark 14:26). Like Mary, they were all Jews, and music was a big part of their religious experience. As Christianity branched off from its Jewish roots, it would retain a lot of the richness of Judaism, including the Jewish Scriptures and the musical element of praising God in worship. An early Christian song made it into St. Paul's Letter to the Philippians around 55 AD, only a couple of decades after the death and resurrection of Jesus. Biblical scholars believe these words may have been part of a hymn about Christ and humility used during those first years of Christian worship:

> Have among yourselves the same attitude that is also
>   yours in Christ Jesus,
> Who, though he was in the form of God,
> did not deem equality with God something to be grasped at.
> Rather, he emptied himself
> And took the form of a slave,
> coming in human likeness.
> He was known to be of human estate,
> and it was thus that he humbled himself,
> obediently accepting even death,
> death on a cross!
> Because of this, God highly exalted him
> and bestowed on him the name
> above every other name,
> so that at Jesus' name
> every knee must bend,
> in the heavens, on the earth, and under the earth,
> and every tongue proclaim
> to the glory of God the Father:
> JESUS CHRIST IS LORD.   *Philippians 2:5–11*

The Church has been making music right from the beginning. St. Isidore of Seville said that a choir is like a crown around the altar. A lot of famous classical music is based on the Bible. Some of the greatest composers wrote music for celebrating Mass. To this day, musicians of every type compose, play, and sing songs as a way of glorifying God. It is almost impossible to imagine celebrating great holy days like Christmas, Easter, and Pentecost (the day the Holy Spirit came down upon the disciples) without music. After all, God, who is Love, is inviting us into an eternal love affair, and as St. Augustine said, "Singing belongs to one who loves."

Praying with the Bible

1 INVITE THE HOLY SPIRIT

Come, O Holy Spirit! Bless us with your presence made known by the Fruits of the Spirit, especially Joy! Even in difficult times, let me know the deep joy that is more lasting than the world's fleeting pleasures. Help me to have joy in my soul to sing, in good times and in bad, trusting always in your help and in your love. (Pause in silence.) (Now read the passage…)

> *While they were eating, [Jesus] took bread, said the blessing, broke it, and gave it to them, and said, "Take it; this is my body." Then he took a cup, gave thanks, and gave it to them, and they all drank from it. He said to them, "This is my blood of the covenant, which will be shed for many. Amen, I say to you, I shall not drink again the fruit of the vine until the day when I drink it new in the kingdom of God." Then, after singing a hymn, they went out to the Mount of Olives.* MARK 14:22-26

2 TALK TO JESUS

Now, talk to Jesus as a friend, in your own words, from your heart. Let him know about what you're going through, whether good or bad. Ask him to be your constant companion through it all. He knows the worst of human experiences. He understands us completely.

3 GIVE GLORY TO THE FATHER

At the Last Supper, Jesus gave us the Eucharist as a way to receive his life into our own. By receiving Holy Communion, we are joined to Christ and one another, like grains of wheat baked together into one bread. There is nothing we do that gives more glory to the Father than to receive the Body and Blood of Christ at Mass and then to live in the world in unity with Christ. Have you received Communion lately? Do you do so regularly? Do you let it change you, so that your communion with Christ draws you into communion with all of creation, especially with the poor and marginalized?

Confirmed in the Faith

QUESTIONS TO HELP US GROW STRONGER

Pick one or two questions to reflect on as you think about the meaning of your Confirmation and life in the Spirit.

- Do you have any musical talents (composing, playing an instrument, singing) that you could share with the church community to enhance our worship together?

- Why do you think music is so important to worship?

- Imagine an age before most people were literate. What role do you think music and the arts played in helping them to know the Bible?

My Bible Journal

A SPACE FOR PERSONAL REFLECTIONS

_____

_____

_____

_____

_____

_____

_____

*"The musical tradition of the universal Church
is a treasure of inestimable value..."*
VATICAN II, SACROSANCTUM CONCILIUM, 112; CCC, 1156

Part III

MAJOR THEMES *of* OUR LOVE SONG TOGETHER

The celestial treasure of the Sacred Books, so bountifully bestowed upon [us] by the Holy Spirit, should not lie neglected." **POPE LEO XIII**

"In God's word, we find many expressions of his love. It is as if he tried to find different ways of showing that love, so that, with one of them at least, he could touch your heart."

POPE FRANCIS

CHAPTER 14

Big Themes of the Bible 1: Creation

"The Bible is not a natural science textbook, nor does it intend to be such. It is a religious book....One cannot get from it a scientific explanation of how the world arose; one can only glean religious experience from it." **CARDINAL JOSEPH RATZINGER**

I n the mid-1800s in what is now the Czech Republic, a monk named Gregor Mendel began experimenting with peas in his garden. His careful observations led him to record some of the rules of heredity, which you may have studied in biology class. For that reason, this Catholic monk is called the Father of Genetics. At about the same time, Charles Darwin introduced his understanding of the origin of species. From these scientific ideas and others, evolutionary biology was born.

In reaction to Darwin's research, some Christians became fundamentalists. They broke with the long tradition of the Church concerning the way to read the Bible. Instead of following St. Augustine's rules, they insisted on reading everything in the Bible literally. They believed it was the word of God without any errors, as if it had been dictated by God. The Catholic Church rejects fundamentalism. Jesus did not read the Bible literally, and neither do we.

So what do Catholics believe about the stories of creation in Genesis, the first book of the Bible? Did God take six days to create the world and then rest on the seventh day? Did God really create Adam from the dust and breathe into his nostrils to make him alive? Did God literally take a rib from Adam to create Eve? The short answer is no. We do not read the stories of creation in the Bible as scientific explanations or as history. The Bible doesn't tell us how the world was made, or how long it took. It doesn't tell us how things evolved or how long ago. Cardinal Ratzinger (the future Pope Benedict XVI) says, "The Scripture would not wish to inform us about how the different species of plant life gradually appeared or how the sun and the moon and the stars were established. Its purpose ultimately would be to say one thing: *God* created the world." In other words, the Bible tells us *who* created the world, not *how*.

Catholics accept the truths that science uncovers. We accept that God is the Creator, and we accept that evolution is part of God's creation. We believe that all truth leads to God. We know from hard experience that when we fall into reading the Bible literally and fail to learn from science (as we did when the Church condemned Galileo for example), we fail to honor God, who gave us the minds to explore the universe. In short, Catholics believe in faith and reason. The Bible helps us to grow in our faith, but it is not a science textbook or a history book. It helps us to know God better. The creation stories are not to be read literally. They are stories meant to fill us with Wonder and Awe, just as science and exploration fill us with Wonder and Awe. That sense of wonder is a gift of the Spirit that points us to the Creator. The creation stories in the Bible want us to know that, "in the beginning...." there is only God, and God created everything out of sheer love.

Praying with the Bible

1 INVITE THE HOLY SPIRIT

Come, O Holy Spirit! Make your presence known by developing in us the Fruit of the Spirit that we call Patience. Give us patience with our human ignorance and limitations as we continue to learn about God's creation through the arts and sciences. (*Pause in silence.*) (*Now read the passage…*)

> *In the beginning was the Word,*
> *and the Word was with God,*
> *and the Word was God.*
> *He was in the beginning with God.*
> *All things came to be through him,*
> *and without him nothing came to be.*
> *What came to be through him was life,*
> *and this life was the light of the human race;*
> *the light shines in the darkness,*
> *and the darkness has not overcome it.* JOHN 1:1-5

2 TALK TO JESUS

Now, talk to Jesus as a friend, in your own words, from your heart. Since he is the true "Word" of God, who embodies all the love that God speaks to the world, entrust all your concerns to him. He will be the light that shines in your own darkness, and that darkness cannot overcome him!

3 GIVE GLORY TO THE FATHER

In 2000, Pope St. John Paul II officially apologized for the Catholic Church's condemnation of Galileo. His apology reminds us that we are not perfect, not even the Church. The Father is glorified when we admit our sins and mistakes and ask forgiveness. Galileo was right to defend the scientific truth that the sun, not the earth, is the center of the solar system. He was also right about the Bible. He said that the Bible was written to "teach us how to go to heaven and not how the heavens go." He understood that human intelligence is a gift from

God: "I am infinitely grateful to God," he said, "who has deigned to choose me alone to be the first to observe such marvelous things which have lain hidden for all ages past." Whatever field we go into, we can recognize God's gift to us, and use our intelligence, our creativity, and our work to give glory to God.

Confirmed in the Faith

QUESTIONS TO HELP US GROW STRONGER

Pick one or two questions to reflect on as you think about the meaning of your Confirmation and life in the Spirit.

- If the creation stories in the Bible aren't literally true, why are they in the Bible?

- Why do you think the Catholic Church rejects the literal reading of the Bible that fundamentalists support?

- Jesus promised that the Holy Spirit would be given to us "to guide you to all truth" (John 16:13). How does the Spirit work through both faith and reason (or, intelligence, intellect, science, critical thinking) to guide us?

My Bible Journal

A SPACE FOR PERSONAL REFLECTIONS

The fundamentalist approach is dangerous, for it is attractive to people who look to the Bible for ready answers to the problems of life. It can deceive these people, offering them interpretations that are pious but illusory, instead of telling them that the Bible does not necessarily contain an immediate answer to each and every problem. Without saying as much in so many words, fundamentalism actually invites people to a kind of intellectual suicide. It injects into life a false certitude, for it unwittingly confuses the divine substance of the biblical message with what are in fact its human limitations. **THE PONTIFICAL BIBLICAL COMMISSION**

CHAPTER 15

Big Themes of the Bible 2: Redemption

"Then the Lord God said to the snake: Because you have done this, cursed are you among all the animals, tame or wild; On your belly you shall crawl, and dust you shall eat all the days of your life. I will put enmity between you and the woman, and between your offspring and hers; They will strike at your head, while you strike at their heel." **GENESIS 3:14-15**

L ike the stories of creation in the Bible, the story of Adam and Eve is not meant to be read literally. In the ancient world, and in many cultures still, the major way of talking about God was/is to tell stories. Sometimes we call them myths, but that word gets misunderstood to mean fairytales. Jewish stories about God were not fairytales. But they weren't history books either. They were ways of thinking about God. In other words, through stories they were doing theology. We shouldn't read those stories literally, but we should ask the Spirit to help us understand the truth about God that is in the stories. And so we don't take literally the Garden of Eden, the talking snake, and the forbidden fruit. These are just elements of the story used to teach a deeper truth.

The main theme of the story of Adam and Eve is sin and the promise of redemption. Cardinal Ratzinger says, "The account tells us that sins begets sin, and that therefore all the sins of history are interlinked." The story, then, is based on a historical truth. Our first human parents, whom the story calls Adam and Eve, were also the first to sin. And from that time until this day, sin has led to more sin.

The story tells us that the serpent tempted them to "be like gods" (Gen 3:5). The serpent is a symbol of Satan to us today, but to the original Jewish audience, the serpent was also a symbol of the fertility cults in the ancient world. They knew that there was a temptation to leave God behind and to join these cults. The story was saying that just as our first parents brought sin into the world by turning away from God, the Jews had to be careful not to turn to idols.

The message is the same for us today. "God is love" (1 John 4:8). We sin when we turn away from love and turn to selfishness instead. By doing that, we turn away from God and attempt to "be like gods." According to Cardinal Ratzinger, "The garden is an image of the world, which to humankind is not a wilderness, a danger, or a threat, but a home, which shelters, nourishes, and sustains. It is an expression for a world that bears the imprint of the Spirit, for a world that came into existence in accordance with the will of the Creator." Our sins don't hurt God (we can't hurt God!), but they do hurt us and our ability to live together in peace. In other words, the symbolic Garden of Eden is destroyed by sin.

Lucky for us, that is not the end of the story. God knew we would sin. We didn't catch God off guard. And right from the beginning God revealed the plan for saving us. Read the passage at the top of the chapter. God promised to destroy the snake by sending a woman who together with her Son would crush its head underfoot. Did you ever see a statue of Mary with her foot crushing a snake? She is the promised woman, and Jesus is the Savior whom God planned to send right from the beginning!

Praying with the Bible

1 INVITE THE HOLY SPIRIT

Come, O Holy Spirit! Make known your presence in my life by bringing forth the Fruit of the Spirit called Love. Since love is the opposite of sin, help me to live in love with God and others. (*Pause in silence.*) (*Now read the passage…*)

> *In conclusion, just as through one transgression condemnation came upon all, so through one righteous act acquittal and life came to all. For just as through the disobedience of one person the many were made sinners, so through the obedience of one the many will be made righteous… [W]here sin increased, grace overflowed all the more, so that, as sin reigned in death, grace also might reign through justification for eternal life through Jesus Christ our Lord.* ROMANS 5:18-21

2 TALK TO JESUS

Now, talk to Jesus as a friend, in your own words, from your heart. Express your gratitude for his mercy and forgiveness. And if you're struggling with a sin that is hard to overcome, ask for his grace to overflow and help you to conquer it right away or, like many saints, gradually over time.

3 GIVE GLORY TO THE FATHER

Jesus taught us that forgiveness comes with a condition: we have to forgive others. In the prayer he taught us, we pray to the Father, "forgive us our trespasses as we forgive those who trespass against us." What if we didn't forgive others? We would be praying for God to do the same to us! In the Letter of St. James, we read, "For the judgment is merciless to one who has not shown mercy"; but fortunately, "mercy triumphs over judgment" (James 2:13). And so Jesus said, "Be merciful, just as [also] your Father is merciful" (Luke 6:36), and also, "Blessed are the merciful, for they will be shown mercy" (Matthew 5:7). So if we want to glorify the Father, we must be like

Christ, who was faithful to his own teaching of mercy; for even from the cross he said, "Father, forgive them, they know not what they do" (Luke 23:34).

Confirmed in the Faith

QUESTIONS TO HELP US GROW STRONGER

Pick one or two questions to reflect on as you think about the meaning of your Confirmation and life in the Spirit.

- One problem with reading the story of Adam and Eve literally is that it makes Eve look like the real culprit (and women have been unjustly treated as "the weaker sex" partly because of this interpretation). Is this the point of the story, though?

- In what ways are you tempted to sin? Do you pray to the Holy Spirit for the gift of Good Judgment and Courage/Fortitude (Strength) to overcome temptation?

- The promise of salvation includes not only the coming of Christ, but also the sending of the Holy Spirit, whom we receive in Baptism and Confirmation. Why is the Spirit essential to our salvation?

My Bible Journal

A SPACE FOR PERSONAL REFLECTIONS

"Sin is an abuse of the freedom that God gives to created persons so that they are capable of loving [God] and loving one another." **CCC, 387**

"The account of the fall in Genesis 3 uses figurative language, but affirms a primeval event, a deed that took place at the beginning of the history of [humankind]." **CCC, 390**

CHAPTER 16

Big Themes of the Bible 3: Repentance and Conversion

"After John [the Baptist] had been arrested, Jesus came to Galilee proclaiming the gospel of God: 'This is the time of fulfillment. The kingdom of God is at hand. Repent, and believe in the gospel.'" **MARK 1:14-15**

One thing that most of us learn about love over the course of our lives is that it's not the same as attraction. When we're first attracted to someone, and they reciprocate the feelings, we're head over heels! We are on such a high! We're ecstatic! Some people call it puppy love. Some call it the honeymoon period. It's that early part of a relationship when everything seems perfect. It just feels so right!

But that's not love. Anyone who has gone through a breakup and looks back on the relationship knows that attraction is not the same thing as love. Love is much harder. Ask anyone who has been married for a long time. Attractions come and go, but love promises to stay. Physical attraction rises and falls like a tide, but love stays solid even after the honeymoon period. Attractions are superficial, but love goes to the core. Love is not just a feeling. It requires commitment and self-sacrifice. It has to wrestle against selfishness to put the other person's needs first. Love involves responsibility. Love means learning to communicate and compromise. It means learning to forgive and to accept forgiveness and to keep no tally. In other words, love is so much more than just an attraction. It involves making changes to become a better person, the best person we can be for the one we love. And we need God's help, God's grace. That's why we say one of the Fruits of the Holy Spirit is Love.

God's love song to us in Scripture is likewise not just about feeling good. God is calling us to real love, the kind that Jesus demonstrated by being willing even to die for us. That kind of love involves conversion. Jesus didn't just say, "Believe in the Good News!" ("good news" is what the word "gospel" means.) Jesus also said, "Repent!" Conversion means repenting of our sins, turning away from selfishness, and letting God teach us how to love. It is one of the major themes of the Bible.

We see this theme, for example, in the story of Noah's Ark (Genesis, chapters 6–9). There may well have been a real Noah and a real flood, but the story isn't meant to be read literally. It's not a history book. Think about the devastating floods and damage from Hurricane Maria in Puerto Rico in 2017. In a pre-scientific world, people would use stories to make sense of it all. There are lots of ancient flood stories. You might have learned about one of the oldest ones in *The Epic of Gilgamesh*.

We know right away not to read the Noah's Ark story literally because it starts by saying that God regretted creating people because of their sins (Genesis 6:6). God doesn't regret anything. Regret implies making a mistake, and God doesn't make mistakes. God knew we would sin, and God planned to send a Savior right from the start.

Jesus used the story as a warning to repent before it is too late (Matthew 14:36–44). The early Christians understood it as an *allegory*, a story that has a hidden meaning that only with Christ became clear. To them, just as in the story God destroys the sinners in a flood, God washes away sin with the waters of Baptism (1 Peter 3:21). And just as in the story, the ark saved Noah and his family, early Christians saw the ark as a symbol of the Church. When we are in the Church, we are saved. Love requires us to convert, to reject sin before it is too late. How do we do that? Through the waters of Baptism! And if we still sin after that, as we all do, then we stay in the Church through the sacrament of Reconciliation (confession). The Church will be the ark that saves us from sin!

Praying with the Bible

1 INVITE THE HOLY SPIRIT

Come, O Holy Spirit! Bless me with your gift of Good Judgment so that all my decisions may help me to enter the Kingdom of God. (*Pause in silence.*) (*Now read the passage…*)

> Then Jesus went through the towns and villages, teaching the people. He was on his way to Jerusalem. Someone asked him, "Lord, are only a few people going to be saved?" He said to them, "Try very hard to enter through the narrow door. I tell you, many will try to enter and will not be able to. The owner of the house will get up and close the door. Then you will stand outside knocking and begging. You will say, 'Sir, open the door for us.' But he will answer, 'I don't know you. And I don't know where you come from.' Then you will say, 'We ate and drank with you. You taught in our streets.' But he will reply, 'I don't know you. And I don't know where you come from. Get away from me, all you who do evil!' You will weep and grind your teeth together when you see those who are in God's kingdom. You will see Abraham, Isaac and Jacob and all the prophets there. But you yourselves will be thrown out. People will come from east and west and north and south. They will take their places at the feast in God's kingdom.
> Then the last will be first. And the first will be last." LUKE 13:22-30

2 TALK TO JESUS

Now, talk to Jesus as a friend, in your own words, from your heart. Express your desire to be part of the Kingdom of God. Examine your conscience. In what ways do you still need to repent?

3 GIVE GLORY TO THE FATHER

When God sees us at the judgment, we do not want to be among those "who do evil" and get cast out. Pray the Our Father slowly and with concentration. We are asking to be delivered from evil.

Confirmed in the Faith

QUESTIONS TO HELP US GROW STRONGER

Pick one or two questions to reflect on as you think about the meaning of your Confirmation and life in the Spirit.

- The story of the flood is meant to remind us how serious sin is. The Holy Spirit will help us to see our sins clearly and to grow in faithfulness. That is why Faithfulness is called a Fruit of the Holy Spirit. In what ways have you grown in faithfulness?

- The whole love song that is the Bible is about God's willingness to forgive us, redeem us, and share eternal life with us. The beginning of that life is having the Holy Spirit in our souls even now. How are you living out Jesus' command to "repent and believe in the gospel" so that you make your soul a welcome dwelling place for the Spirit?

- How is love different from puppy love or just attraction? How does knowing the difference help us to think about our love for God?

My Bible Journal

A SPACE FOR PERSONAL REFLECTIONS

_____

_____

"The New Testament is hidden in the Old and the Old is made manifest in the New." **ST. AUGUSTINE**

CHAPTER 17

Big Themes of the Bible 4: Freedom and Covenant

"My love for the Bible goes back a long way. I stutter. I always have, and I guess I always will. As a young boy I read in a newspaper that Moses stuttered. I looked it up in the Bible, and sure enough in Exodus 4:10 Moses says to God: 'I am slow of speech and slow of tongue.' But I found much more in Exodus 3—4. It is the story of God's self-revelation to Moses at Mount Horeb. It tells about the burning bush, the suffering of God's people Israel in Egypt, ...[and] God's promise of liberation from slavery..." **FR. DANIEL HARRINGTON, SJ**

There is no love without freedom. This is true in human relationships and with God. No matter how much we like somebody else, it is just an infatuation if they don't freely respond with the same feelings. When the other person in freedom rejects us, it hurts, but the right thing to do is to accept it. We don't retaliate. We don't spread rumors or begin cyberbullying. We don't violate their freedom with unwanted advances and stalking. It's called respect, and it requires Self-control, which is one of the Fruits of the Holy Spirit.

God shows respect to us as well. God offers love but doesn't force it. Instead, God respects our freedom. Unfortunately, if we use our freedom to reject God, we are also rejecting love and life itself, for "God is love" (1 John 4:8). Rejecting God in an ultimate way would be hell, quite literally. God never sends anyone to hell, but God does not force anyone into love. An eternal rejection of love is one definition of hell. This doesn't mean all atheists or non-Catholics go to hell. It's much deeper than that. Choosing hell means rejecting what God is—love itself. Jesus didn't say our judgment would be based on whether we believed in God in some intellectual way. He said it would be based on whether we did the things love does: feeding the hungry, giving a drink to the thirsty, clothing the naked, taking care of the sick, visiting those in prison, and welcoming the stranger (Matthew 25:31ff). On the flip side, he also warned, "Not everyone who says to me, 'Lord, Lord,' will enter the kingdom of heaven, but only the one who does the will of my Father in heaven" (Matt 7:21).

Since love requires freedom, God is the first defender of freedom. The Exodus story is the most important story to this day for Jews, and since Jesus, Mary, and the disciples were all Jews, this story is central to Christianity as well. When the Israelites were enslaved in Egypt, God sent Moses to deliver them out of slavery. Defending freedom, human rights, and human dignity remain a key part of Catholic social teaching.

After freeing the slaves, God then gives Moses the Ten Commandments and offers to form a covenant with the people. A covenant is like a marriage contract. It is, like love itself, a two-way street. For those who accept the covenant, their responsibility is to live by the commandments. In the end, Jesus is the only one who lives the commandments perfectly, and he completes the marriage of humanity with God. In marriage, the two become one. When Jesus offers us his Spirit in the sacrament of Confirmation, it is to join us to himself and to draw us into the marriage with God. He is offering perfect love, which is eternal life and happiness. But it's only an offer. We are free to accept it or reject it. Confirmation is an invitation, not an obligation.

Praying with the Bible

1 INVITE THE HOLY SPIRIT

Come, O Holy Spirit! Fill me with the gifts of Good Judgment and Wisdom to decide well how to use my freedom. Let me know your presence by experiencing the Fruits of the Spirit called Goodness and Generosity. *(Pause in silence.) (Now read the passage…)*

> *God called out to him from the bush: Moses! Moses! He answered, "Here I am." God said: Do not come near! Remove your sandals from your feet, for the place where you stand is holy ground. I am the God of your father, he continued, the God of Abraham, the God of Isaac, and the God of Jacob. Moses hid his face, for he was afraid to look at God. But the LORD said: I have witnessed the affliction of my people in Egypt and have heard their cry against their taskmasters, so I know well what they are suffering. Therefore I have come down to rescue them from the power of the Egyptians and lead them up from that land into a good and spacious land, a land flowing with milk and honey… Now indeed the outcry of the Israelites has reached me, and I have seen how the Egyptians are oppressing them. Now, go! I am sending you to Pharaoh to bring my people, the Israelites, out of Egypt.* EXODUS 3:4-10

2 TALK TO JESUS

Now, talk to Jesus as a friend, in your own words, from your heart. As the Israelites cried out to God from their slavery, talk to Jesus about your burdens. He will not leave you alone. Don't be afraid to ask others for help too—even as he carried his cross, Jesus had Simon of Cyrene to help him and Veronica to wipe his face. Talk to Jesus about whom you can ask for help.

3 GIVE GLORY TO THE FATHER.

The commandments do not make us slaves to God. That would be too ironic. Instead, God gave them as a way to keep us free. We give glory to the Father by obeying the commandments because they are God's blueprint to keeping us from being slaves to sin and selfishness.

Confirmed in the Faith

QUESTIONS TO HELP US GROW STRONGER

Pick one or two questions to reflect on as you think about the meaning of your Confirmation and life in the Spirit.

- Scripture is full of reminders about those days in slavery. God says in various ways: You were once treated like slaves in a foreign land—don't do that to others! How can you stand against various forms of slavery today, and stand up for freedom, human dignity, and human rights?

- How well do you live out the Ten Commandments? Where are you strongest? Where are you weakest? Ask God to grow in Faithfulness, one of the Fruits of the Holy Spirit.

- How can we help others to see that God does not want us to live in slavery, but to be free? A lot of people think that religion and the commandments take away from our freedom. Do you agree?

My Bible Journal

A SPACE FOR PERSONAL REFLECTIONS

_____

_____

_____

"To listen to sacred Scripture and then to practice mercy: this is the great challenge before us in life. God's word has the power to open our eyes and to enable us to renounce a stifling and barren individualism and instead to embark on a new path of sharing and solidarity." **POPE FRANCIS**

CHAPTER 18

Big Themes of the Bible 5: Justice and Peace

"You have been told, O mortal, what is good,
and what the LORD requires of you:
Only to do justice and to love goodness,
and to walk humbly with your God." **MICAH 6:8**

In the last chapter, we talked about God's covenant with the Israelites freed from slavery. We said it was like a marriage contract, and both sides had to say, in a sense, "I do." Keeping the commandments was both a way to show love for God and a God-given way to learn how to live in freedom. Worshiping God through rituals and sacrifices was another way to show love for God. The point of a sacrifice was to offer God the best portion of what the people had, whether from their herds or from their fields. It involved offering it to God on an altar, and then typically eating the offerings. We don't practice animal sacrifice in most places today, so these ancient rituals sound very strange to us. The best modern equivalent might be saying Grace, or a blessing, before meals. The meat and the vegetables we eat have been sacrificed, in a sense, for our nourishment. Saying a blessing reminds us to be grateful.

Over time, God reveals through the prophets that God is not pleased with the rituals and sacrifices because the prayer has become hypocritical. The people were claiming to worship God, but they were not taking care of one another. Later, for the new Christian communities, St. John would write, "If anyone says, 'I love God,' but hates his brother [or sister], he is a liar; for whoever does not love a brother [or sister] whom he has seen cannot love God whom he has not seen" (1 John 4:20). Both the Old Testament and the New Testament reveal that what God really wants is people to be treated fairly—in other words: justice.

When I think of justice, I think of the prophets. Sometimes people think prophets were people who foretold the future. Usually, though, prophets were called by God to speak the truth that others didn't want to hear. They were often despised because they stood up for justice and peace. A modern-day example would be Martin Luther King Jr. Although his Christian message was about justice and his methods were non-violent, he was still hated by many and ultimately assassinated. Being a prophet takes real Courage, one of the gifts of the Holy Spirit.

A major prophet in the Bible was Isaiah. Listen to what God said through Isaiah: "What do I care for the multitude of your sacrifices? says the Lord....In the blood of calves, lambs, and goats I find no pleasure.... When you spread out your hands, I will close my eyes to you; Though you pray the more, I will not listen. Your hands are full of blood! Wash yourselves clean! Put away your misdeeds from before my eyes; cease doing evil; learn to do good. Make justice your aim: redress the wronged, hear the orphan's plea, defend the widow" (Isaiah 1:11, 15–17). Orphans and widows had very little power in that society, and so they were vulnerable to abuse. The prophets repeatedly named four groups that God wanted the people to care for in a special way: widows, orphans, the poor, and immigrants.

To this day, the words of the prophets ring true. Although we should go to church and participate in our own rituals, God still makes clear that we are hypocrites if we don't also care for the poor, the vulnerable, the immigrants, and the marginalized among us. Pope Francis said, for example, "It's hypocrisy to call yourself a Christian and chase away a refugee." The music of the love song is spoiled if it is not backed up by these concrete acts of love and mercy. That is why God said through Amos the prophet: "Take away from me your noisy songs; The melodies of your harps, I will not listen to them. Rather let justice surge like waters, and righteousness like an unfailing stream" (Amos 5:23–24). To respond faithfully to the word of God, we must be committed to justice and peace in the world, caring especially for those who are most powerless and in need.

Using a different translation of the prophet Micah than the one at the start of this chapter, we hear God telling us that what is good and what is required of us is only this: "to act justly and to love mercy and to walk humbly with your God." Sometimes people think that justice is about vengeance. But the prophet connects justice with mercy. Pope Francis tells us: "mercy is the fullness of justice and the most radiant manifestation of God's truth." He says it is "the key to heaven." No wonder Jesus said, "Blessed are the merciful" in the same breath as saying "Blessed are the peacemakers" and "Blessed are those who hunger and thirst for justice" (Matthew 5:3ff).

Praying with the Bible

1 INVITE THE HOLY SPIRIT

Come, O Holy Spirit! Fill me with your gift of Courage so that I may speak out against injustice and work tirelessly for peace in the world. (*Pause in silence.*) (*Now read the passage…*)

> [Jesus] came to Nazareth, where he had grown up, and went according to his custom into the synagogue on the Sabbath day. He stood up to read and was handed a scroll of the prophet Isaiah. He unrolled the scroll and found the passage where it was written:
>
> "The Spirit of the Lord is upon me,
> because he has anointed me
> to bring glad tidings to the poor.
> He has sent me to proclaim liberty to captives
> and recovery of sight to the blind,
> to let the oppressed go free,
> and to proclaim a year acceptable to the Lord."…
>
> He said to them, "Today this scripture passage is fulfilled in your hearing." **LUKE 4:16-21**

2 TALK TO JESUS

Now, talk to Jesus as a friend, in your own words, from your heart. Bring to him the oppressed people of the world. There is still so much racial injustice, for example, and the U.S. bishops remind us that "Racism is not merely one sin among many; it is a radical evil." There is also terrible poverty, homophobia, sexism, anti-immigrant sentiment, anti-Semitism, and Islamophobia. At your school, there may be bullying based on these things or other injustices like them. Talk to Jesus about what to do. Ask for his help.

3 GIVE GLORY TO THE FATHER

In the sacrament of Confirmation, the Spirit of the Lord will come upon you just as the Spirit was with Jesus in the passage above. Ask the Spirit to help you to continue Jesus' work of bringing "glad tidings to the poor" and helping the "oppressed go free." These are actions that glorify the Father.

Confirmed in the Faith

QUESTIONS TO HELP US GROW STRONGER

Pick one or two questions to reflect on as you think about the meaning of your Confirmation and life in the Spirit.

- Why do you think the gift of Courage is so necessary for anyone who wants to be a follower of Christ?

- Catholics say the "Two Feet" of Catholic Social Teaching that we need to move ahead in love are works of justice and works of charity. What does each "foot" require of us?

- St. Catherine of Siena said, "We've had enough exhortations to be silent. Cry out with a thousand tongues—I see the world is rotten because of silence." What do you think she meant?

- What organizations can help me to get involved in the work of justice and peace?

My Bible Journal
A SPACE FOR PERSONAL REFLECTIONS

_____

_____

_____

_____

_____

"Human interdependence is increasing and gradually spreading throughout the world. The unity of the human family, embracing people who enjoy equal natural dignity, implies a universal common good. This good calls for the organization of the community of nations able to 'provide for the different needs of [people; such as] ...food, hygiene, education, ...alleviating the miseries of refugees,...and assisting migrants and their families.'"

CATECHISM OF THE CATHOLIC CHURCH, 1911

CHAPTER 19

Big Themes of the Bible 6: Mission and Mercy

"Sacred Scripture accomplishes its prophetic work above all in those who listen to it. It proves bitter and sweet....The sweetness of God's word leads us to share it with all those whom we encounter in this life and to proclaim the sure hope that it contains (cf. 1 Pet. 3:15–16). Its bitterness, in turn, often comes from our realization of how difficult it is to live that word consistently, or our personal experience of seeing it rejected as meaningless for life." **POPE FRANCIS**

Have you ever had a friend who fell into puppy love and just wouldn't stop talking about the person they were dating? No matter what you talk about, suddenly they've managed to say something about their boyfriend or girlfriend (or this person they hope will become their boyfriend or girlfriend). They want to show you pictures like crazy. All of their social media is filled with just this one theme. It's like they never stop thinking about their loved one.

When puppy love gives way to real love, this phenomenon doesn't go away. The giddiness goes away, but the thoughtfulness doesn't. Spouses have each other on their minds all the time. Parents have their children on their minds all the time. Even animal lovers spend the day at work or school just waiting to get home to their dogs and cats.

If God's love story turns us into lovers of God, one thing we can expect for sure is that the signs of both puppy love and deep love will be present. We won't be able to hide our love! It will spill over into everything we do. The Jesuit priest Fr. Pedro Arrupe put it this way:

> Nothing is more practical than finding God, than falling in Love in a quite absolute, final way. What you are in love with, what seizes your imagination, will affect everything. It will decide what will get you out of bed in the morning, what you do with your evenings, how you spend your weekends, what you read, whom you know, what breaks your heart, and what amazes you with joy and gratitude.
>
> Fall in Love, stay in love, and it will decide everything.

The way our love for God shows itself is in prayer and in service, especially in the Works of Mercy. Jesus' mission from the Father was to reconcile the world to God. His mission was mercy. In Confirmation, we accept his Spirit and his mission. Pope Francis reminds us that it begins with the Church: "No one can be excluded from the mercy of God. The Church is the house where everyone is welcomed and no one is rejected." We have to make that a reality. But then, we have to go out beyond the Church into the world and share the Good News of God's mercy, the Good News of salvation. We do that more by witness than by words. As St. Francis of Assisi is often reported to have said: "Preach the gospel in everything you do. If necessary, use words."

The Works of Mercy include feeding the hungry, taking care of the sick, praying for the living and the dead, forgiving offenses, helping the homeless, and (a new one Pope Francis added) caring for the environment. You should look up the full list. Together with the many works of justice and peace, the Works of Mercy are part of the mission of the Church. By living according to them, we are living out our love of God. "You are the light of the world." Jesus said, "A city set on a mountain cannot be hidden. Nor do they light a lamp and then put it under a bushel basket; it is set on a lampstand, where it gives light to all in the house. Just so, your light must shine before others, that they may see your good deeds and glorify your heavenly Father" (Matthew 5:14–16). By those good deeds and that light shared in a world that is sometimes very dark, we are evangelizing, which means sharing the gospel with others. By word and deed, we invite them to hear God's love song and to join us in falling in love with God.

Praying with the Bible

1 INVITE THE HOLY SPIRIT

Come, O Holy Spirit! Give me ears to hear how God is calling me to show my love and to continue Christ's mission of mercy. *(Pause in silence.) (Now read the passage…)*

> *On the evening of that first day of the week, when the doors were locked, where the disciples were, for fear of the [other] Jews, Jesus came and stood in their midst and said to them, "Peace be with you." When he had said this, he showed them his hands and his side. The disciples rejoiced when they saw the Lord. [Jesus] said to them again, "Peace be with you. As the Father has sent me, so I send you." And when he had said this, he breathed on them and said to them, "Receive the holy Spirit. Whose sins you forgive are forgiven them, and whose sins you retain are retained."*
>
> **JOHN 20:19-23**

2 TALK TO JESUS

Now, talk to Jesus as a friend, in your own words, from your heart. What are your dreams? How would you like to make the world better? What gifts are you discovering in yourself that can be used to serve others? Ask him how you can join in his mission of mercy.

3 GIVE GLORY TO THE FATHER.

St. Katharine Drexel said, "It is a lesson we all need—to let alone the things that do not concern us. He has other ways for others to follow Him; all do not go by the same path. It is for each of us to learn the path by which He requires us to follow Him, and to follow Him in that path." It is the same theme that the Trappist monk, Thomas Merton, wrote about: "To me to be a saint is to be myself." He taught us that we give glory to the Father by being truly ourselves, and not giving in to being fake. This is also what St. Catherine of Siena meant when she said, "Be who God meant you to be and you will set the world on fire." The imagery comes from Jesus himself, who said he came to set the world afire (Luke 12:49). The fire is the Holy Spirit! It is God's love! Give glory to the Father by being truly whom God created you to be, and set others aflame with love.

Confirmed in the Faith

QUESTIONS TO HELP US GROW STRONGER

Pick one or two questions to reflect on as you think about the meaning of your Confirmation and life in the Spirit.

- What do you think Fr. Arrupe meant when he said, "Nothing is more practical than finding God, than falling in Love in a quite absolute, final way"?

- Do you agree that when you're really in love it shows in both words and actions?

- Have you thought about Confirmation based on the reading on the previous page, where Jesus says, "As the Father has sent me, so I send you" and breathes on them his Holy Spirit?

My Bible Journal

A SPACE FOR PERSONAL REFLECTIONS

_____

_____

"The person who thirsts for God eagerly studies and meditates on the inspired word, knowing that there [they are] certain to find the one for whom [they] thirst."

ST. BERNARD OF CLAIRVAUX

CHAPTER 20

Resources for Further Learning

"The Holy Spirit has, with admirable wisdom and care for our welfare, so arranged the Holy Scriptures as by the plainer passages to satisfy our hunger, and by the more obscure to stimulate our appetite." **ST. AUGUSTINE**

God's Word is a living word, not a dead text. For that reason, there will never be a time in the Church's history when we are not still listening to and learning what God is saying to us in the Bible. Nobody has it all figured out! As Thomas Groome says, "Nobody's word is the last word on God's Word." That would be impossible, since God is still speaking. To help us in reading Scripture properly, with a soul open to hearing the living Word of God, the Church recommends various resources to us. Here are several to help you continue to grow in faith as a follower of Christ Jesus, who is the Word of God made flesh.

"Hearing the word of God with reverence and proclaiming it with faith...this present council [Vatican II] wishes to set forth authentic doctrine on divine revelation...**so that by hearing the message of salvation the whole world may believe, by believing it may hope, and by hoping it may love.**"

DEI VERBUM, THE DOGMATIC CONSTITUTION ON DIVINE REVELATION, 1

SUGGESTED RESOURCES

Stephen J. Binz, ***Threshold to God's Word: A User Friendly Guide to Scripture Study***

Stephen J. Binz, ***Threshold Bible Study*** (series)

Michael Carotta, ***Spirit and Truth: A Self-Guided Scripture Study for Confirmation and Beyond***

Margarget Nutting Ralph, ***Scripture Basics: A Catechist's Guide***

The Catholic Youth Bible

The Catholic Study Bible, 3rd edition (Oxford University Press)

Vatican II document, ***Dei Verbum*** (Dogmatic Constitution on Divine Revelation)

Catechism of the Catholic Church

Pope Benedict XVI, ***Verbum Domini*** (The Word of the Lord)

The Pontifical Biblical Commission, ***The Interpretation of the Bible in the Church***

Daniel Harrington, SJ, ***How Catholics Read the Bible***

The New Jerome Biblical Commentary

The ***Sacra Pagina*** series of New Testament commentaries (Liturgical Press)

OF RELATED INTEREST

Hearts on Fire

*A Guide to Catholic
Spirituality for Teens*

MARGARET FELICE

This clear and succinct book invites teens to consider the many ways we grow spiritually: through the sacraments, prayer, and attentiveness to God's presence in everyday occurrences. As teens explore these Catholic spiritual practices and approaches to living, they'll discover new ways to grow in faith and how they can stay open to their need for God throughout their lives.

32 PAGES | $3.95 | 5½" X 8½"
9781627855426

Spirit, Show Me the Way

*Confirmation Prayers based
on the Fruits of the Holy Spirit*

MARGARET FELICE

This beautiful book of prayers is tuned to the many emotions, needs, anxieties, experiences, and challenges that teens face as they navigate their complex, rapidly changing world. Based on the twelve Fruits of the Holy Spirit, each prayer helps teens get a glimpse of the possibilities that await when they open their hearts to the grace of the Holy Spirit working within them.

64 PAGES | $8.95 | 4" X 6"
9781627855457